Cpt. Rattan Singh Pal

Indian Family Tree

Tony's Parents

Tony

Indian Family Tree

Tony & Rani

Prince

Indian Family Tree

Tony's Daughters

Chandigarh City

House of Hope & Health Clinic with Sunny & Karin

House of Hope

Benjamin & Joseph

Children & Teachers

Title

India Beckons

by

Dorothy Fallows - Thompson

I.S.B.N. 978-0-244-04492-3

Copyright © 2017 Dorothy Fallows -Thompson

All rights reserved, including the right to reproduce this book, or portions thereof in any form. No part of this text maybe reproduced, transmitted, downloaded, decompiled, reverse engineered, or stored, in any form or introduced into any means, whether electronic or mechanical without the express written permission of the author.

Published by: Dorothy Fallows -Thompson

Sub Title

India Beckons

Sequel to

'For the Love of a Boy'

The on-going saga of a life changing adventure

India.

Bible Translations Used Copyright List.

Holy Bible Copyright for Translations used in this book. THE HOLY BIBLE, NEW INTERNATIONAL VERSION®, NIV® Copyright © 1973, 1978, 1984, 2011 by Biblical®.

Amplified Bible (AMP)Copyright © 1954, 1958, 1962, 1964, 1965, 1987 by The Lockman Foundation

Complete Jewish Bible (CJB) Copyright © 1998 by David H. Stern. All rights reserved.

Arabic Bible: Easy-to-Read Version (ERV-AR), Arabic Life Application Bible (ALAB) .. Copyright ©2009 World Bible Translation Centre.

Easy-to-Read Version (ERV) Copyright © 2006 by World Bible Translation Centre.

AENT Aramaic English New Testament Copyright: Glenn David Bauscher (Standard Copyright License

GOD'S WORD® *is a copyrighted work of God's Word to the Nations. Copyright © 1995 by God's Word to the Nations. All rights reserved. Used by permission. Nations. All rights reserved. Used by permission.*

New Living Translation (NLT) Holy Bible. New Living Translation copyright© 1996, 2004, 2007, 2013 by Tyndale House Foundation. Used by permission of Tyndale House Publishers Inc., Carol Stream, Illinois 60188. All rights reserved.

'Dedicated'

To all the wonderful

Children of 'House of Hope'

India

Acknowledgements

I would like to thank first of all, the dedicated staff, friends and precious children of House of Hope', to whom I have dedicated this continuing story of God's love.

Also joyful thanks to my dear friend, Dr. Deirdre Shawe who has written a very informative and insightful foreword for the book. More than words can express gratitude for her continued commitment and dedication to increase the health and welfare of these children and their families.

Grateful thanks once again to all those who have graciously allowed me to tell their story within these pages and I do pray that all will be blessed as they read it.

Massive thanks also, to my family and friends for continued encouragement to relate more of this on-going saga for the Glory of God alone.

More than anything I wish to thank God from the bottom of my heart for all His faithfulness to me throughout my life, way beyond any words I could express.

<blockquote>
Give thanks to the LORD, for he is good!

His faithful love endures forever.

Psalm 136:1 (NLT) Holy Bible
</blockquote>

Foreword

Dr. Deirdre Shawe. MB. BS, FRCP, DCH, MRCGP

This book, written by Dorothy Fallows-Thompson, is a sequel to "For the love of a Boy". The "boy" is Dorothy's "son of the heart", a young Indian man who asked Dorothy to be his mother, when his own mother died, as she had befriended his parents many years previously. This developing mother-son relationship brings Dorothy to India, where she becomes inspired to help the children from the Dalit community otherwise known as the "untouchables", who are the lowest in the Hindu caste system. It took ten years to bring this dream to a reality, with the opening of a school, the House of Hope, in the slum area of Chandigarh, a city in the Punjab, North India.

The Dalit communities are distributed throughout India, but are most common in the Indian Punjab, where they represent almost 30% of the population. They have a long history; a Chinese Buddhist pilgrim, who visited India in the early 4th century, recorded that the Dalits were segregated from the mainstream society as untouchables. They were considered as the fifth group beyond the fourfold division of Indian people. They were not allowed to let their shadow fall upon a non-Dalit caste member and were required to sweep the ground where they had walked to remove the 'contamination' of their footfalls. Dalits were forbidden to worship in temples or draw water from the same wells as caste Hindus, and they usually lived in segregated areas outside the main village. In the Indian countryside, even today, the Dalit villages are usually a separate enclave a kilometer or so outside the main village where the other Hindu castes reside. Although the Indian government has sought to deal with this gross form of inequality in recent years, by making education available to these communities, this project has only been partially successful. In practice, education is not available to many, unless offered by a charitable organization, and children can parents have done, in desperate poverty with limited health care and education, and working throughout their lives in menial tasks such as cleaning public latrines and picking out waste plastic from the city refuse heaps, for recycling. Their only hope is to live a good life so that when they are re-incarnated in the next life they may occupy a higher place in the caste system.

"India beckons" is the ongoing story of the miraculous transformation of a group of Dalit children and their families in the Punjab, brought about by the provision of education, love and care at the House of Hope. It sees these children making a success of their education, giving them the hope of being able to break free from the chains of the caste system. The project has been driven by Dorothy's irrepressible enthusiasm and support, and made possible by the hard work, faith and courage of those who run the school day to day, bringing hope where there was none. It is a light in a dark world and an example of what Jesus promised, in the gospel of Luke, Chapter 4, quoting from the Old Testament: Isaiah Chapter 61: v.1-3: **The Spirit of the Lord is upon me, because the Lord has anointed me to preach the good news to the poor. He has sent me to bind up the broken hearted, to proclaim freedom for the captives and release from darkness for the prisoners to proclaim the year of the Lord's favour and the day of vengeance of our God, to comfort all who mourn, and provide for those who grieve in Zion - to bestow on them a crown of beauty instead of ashes, and the oil of gladness instead of mourning, and the garment of praise instead of a spirit of despair. They will be called oaks of righteousness, a planting of the Lord for the display of his splendour, to preach the good news to the poor.**

In this book, we read the story of these promises coming to fruition in young but precious lives.

Deirdre Shawe

Preface

'India Beckons' This title chosen by Peter (my husband) exactly exemplifies the life changing experience and impact India has had on our lives; and that of many other of our friends, with its power to draw us back there whenever possible.

As related in my first book 'For the Love of a Boy' a chance meeting with an Indian Army Captain more than forty years before started a series of events, where God would lead me to visit North India, intrinsically, interweaving our lives with that of a Hindu family there. This 'Love story' we hope will never end!

God also graciously enabled us to 'help in a small way' other young and needy lives, for the Glory and Honour of His name alone.

As you read these pages, my prayer is that the Risen Christ (my Saviour and Lord) will become your friend too, filling your life with the joy and expectancy, He bestows on me daily, as I surrender my will to His.

Dorothy

Also by the Author

For the Love of a Boy

For the Love of a Boy is the story of the years before *India Beckons*. Here Dorothy relates in her words 'the Miracle of Love' God has done in my heart as a result of a mother's love thousands of miles away from my home'. She tells of her first trip to India, its sights, sounds and lasting impressions, resulting in a lifelong love for India and her people, beginning with a special mother love for a boy and his family.

Life Lines 1 & 2

Religion v Freedom is taken from one of these books of poetry, where Dorothy looks at life's various situations, from God's prospective, as written in the Holy Bible. This she states has brought her peace of mind and renewed strength for daily living.

Religion v Freedom

How can I know the truth for sure?

I grope around sometimes in fear!

Will I do all that the rules demand

To placate my god, made with a man's hand?

...

Or do I serve an *angry god*

who'll always my mistakes record

Will I reach the height of piety? I ask

I'll never know: I get, *No Answers back!*

...

Or is my god a great philosophy

worked out by a man's own ingenuity?

Or do I have no god at all

Although I'm sure: *I'm not sinless,* sometimes I fail.

...

Am I, the king upon *My Throne*

With all the answers mine alone?

When trouble comes, who can touch my soul?

What if I should find there's a *God to Extol?*

...

All these questions flood the enquirer's mind

I'd like to know if there's a god around

Who cares what happens to my soul

I'd like to meet him: *If he's real!*

...

Then one happy, joyful day, I heard

of a God who created our entire Earth.

Such a Mighty, Majestic Lord, He Reigns!

How could I meet *His Holy* terms?

...

He sent *His One, Unique and only Son*

'Jesus the Christ' introduced, as the *One*.

With love so vast, as *God Supreme*

This Jesus died and rose again

...

The reason was to take my sin

And cast it far, that filthy thing.

Covered by His *Death and Rising Again*

Now a *Relationship* is mine to begin.

...

I call out then, *"Oh, Help Me, Lord!*

What do you demand, I do to serve"?

Then in love, I hear an amazing Voice...

"Lay your burden down. You've made your choice

...

Accept My Love so freely given

To turn your life around - Forgiven!

You're now My Friend and Family member.

No need to grovel: just your life to Me Surrender".

...

I took the *Gift of Life* He offered

I thanked *My God*, the *Loving Shepherd*

Now I live closely to His heart

Each day *His Joy* to me imparts.

...

"You are My Own, My Blood-Bought, Mine;

I'll be here to guide you until the end of time

Simply put your hand in Mine to-day

As your Special Name, I love to say

...

It's written by Me there; on My Palm

This Intimate Relationship is God's Plan".

No need to ask, *"Have I done enough"?*

God accepts His Son, *'My Substitute'.*

...

One day I'll meet Jesus - *face to face*

This wonderful Friend so - *full of grace*

All my fears and longings then will be met

As I fall in gratitude, at His feet.

...

Contents

Indian Family Tree

House of Hope

Dedication

Acknowledgements

Foreword

Preface

Poem

Chapter 1   Awakened

Chapter 2   Looking Back - God Connections

Chapter 3   Dreams become Reality

Chapter 4   Changing Times

Chapter 5   Chandigarh Welcomes

Chapter 6   House of Hope Project 2012

Chapter 7   Great Achievements

Chapter 8   New Life Style For us

Chapter 9   Change is Inevitable

...

Chapter 10 Where do we go from here?

Chapter 11 Deirdre Tells Her Story

Chapter 12 Friends of House of Hope

Chapter 13 Amazing Grace

Chapter 14 Moving Forward

Chapter 15 My time at the Farm

Impressions of India by friends

Chapter 1

Awakened!

2012 I wakened early that morning, feeling unsettled, needing to pray. I crept gently out of bed trying not to wake Peter as it was about 3am. *As usual, I thanked God for all His blessings on my life and most of all for Himself and that because of my precious 'Lord and Saviour Jesus Christ' I could come boldly to God and pour out my heart.* My mind quickly remembered that adopted son of my heart, Tony David and his family, in India, and I felt a deep need to pray. It was as ever a very simple prayer *'God Almighty I am so thankful you hear me always, please provide whatever is needed for this family today in the mighty Name of Jesus'.* I felt a deep sadness in my heart, which seemed more so than usual but I knew that God would only wake me and burden my heart when the need was greatest. I logged onto 'Face book' in the evening and chatted with Sapna, (Tony's second daughter).

"Dadi Ji (Grandfather) is a little sick."

Could this be *why* God had called me to pray?

"Please keep in touch let me know how he is, give him our love and God's blessing," I implored.

Soon I was to learn that Rattan Singh Pal had been admitted to hospital very ill. I was able to speak with him and although weak and on oxygen, he managed a whispered *"Hello"*. Shanti, his daughter said he was happy to hear my voice. I was so thankful that I had been able to speak with him briefly a few times after that initial call, giving him some words of blessing from the Bible; *as in a couple of days he had passed away!* He had celebrated his eightieth birthday, therefore had lived to a good age, especially for someone living in India.

This was the end of a lifelong friendship between us. What now of that family who had touched my heart? Would they still want to remain the 'Jewel in the Crown' of my very existence? Only time would tell...

Memories 1971 Rattan Singh Pal

Looking back in my mind's eye to forty odd years before; I could see this tall, slim dark-haired man of military bearing that had been 'Pal'.

I saw scenes of Catterick Camp in Yorkshire, England and in particular the Sandes Soldier's Home, an old mansion with lots of rooms. This was one of many such properties that had been instigated by Miss Elsie Sandes in the 1800's to provide a *'Home from Home'* for young soldiers and airmen.

At that time I had been working as a civilian nursing sister in the military hospital next door to that particular building and frequented the home for coffee and snacks after work, to play Pool or, more often on Sundays, to watch the 'Fact and Faith' films shown for the benefit of everyone. Sandes also provided temporary accommodation for foreign military personnel on assignment to the Catterick Base. This is how *'Pal'* and I had become acquainted as one evening we had invited him to our home for a meal.

(Something we had done similarly many times with others) and Sandra Connor, my closest friend, came too. She and I had become soul mates immediately on our arrival in Catterick in 1970. I'm delighted to say, that connection remains so, these many years later!

Our both families had become friendly with Pal, often meeting at Sandes and taking walks together while Pal pushed David (Sandy's first son) in his pram. At this time Pal often mentioned how much he missed his youngest son Tony, who was then three years old, so before he returned to India he gave me a photograph of his wife and the boy, as a baby, and we agreed to keep in touch.

Over the years we'd updated one another about family and life in general. How little I *then* knew the impact this 'casual friendship' would have on my life.

However, here I was now, having lost a dear and valued friend and left wondering and hoping that this would not be the end of a relationship of love and laughter with his family.

In the 'Hindu' tradition I understood that the cremation takes place as soon as possible, usually within twelve hours of death and lasts until sunset. Afterwards there were many rituals to be observed, most importantly the ashes to be taken to the Ganges River by the male members of the family. Then a huge meal shared with all the extended family. It was also customary to carry out purification for a minimum of thirteen days; donations being given for the poor and needy as part of this thankfulness for the life of the deceased, in this case Rattan Singh Pal.

Vishakha and Rajeev (Pal's grand-daughter and her husband) were living in England at the time, so I went by train to meet up with Vish. (Tony's niece) and we remembered Pal together. This was a very moving day filled with shared loss and deep love between us.

It was some weeks after this before I was able to chat with Tony on the telephone, but I found that *'joy of joys'* our relationship was still that of *'mother and son'*.

Obviously, Tony was sad at the loss of his aged father, who had been a stalwart of the family, especially since Tony's *only son* Prince had been drowned in a freak accident during his summer holidays, three years previously, in 2009, as related in my first book about India.

'I must mention the wonderful kindness of Rev. Ian Bentley who allowed me to launch the above named book at Christ Church in April 2013 prior to leaving the UK. Giving me the opportunity to tell of the amazing things God had done for me, while at the same time promoting the 'House of Hope' charity'.

Our major decision to move abroad had been made in a matter of months as Peter's health had been deteriorating and the *Ataxia Cerebella,* from which he suffered, had become more troublesome. So he'd made a quick decision to finish work at his part-time retirement job as caretaker at Christ Church.

Although he had thoroughly enjoyed working at the church and meeting so many special people every day; especially the indomitable ladies at 'Coffee & Co' who had treated him every Monday to delicious homemade cakes, *even this,* couldn't keep him there, as he now felt his limitations.

The previous year he had to retire early from full-time employment as he no longer felt able to fulfil his role to *his satisfaction,* as this involved a lot of Crown Court work and telephone interaction. Leaving this job was traumatic for him as he had never been out of work, since the age of fifteen, when he had joined the Royal Navy.

Nevertheless we *now* anticipated a new and exciting outdoor life in Majorca, one of the Balearic Islands, off the coast of mainland Spain.

The tragic death of Prince (Tony's only son) in 2009 had affected Tony badly and he had continued to drink heavily prior to his father's illness. However, now on the death of his father, he had taken charge of all the care and arrangements for Pal's funeral; the shock of which apparently giving him the impetus to resume responsibility for his household once again. How Peter and I thanked God for this, in spite of all the sadness we felt at Pal's death.

Somehow, we reflected together, *Rattan Singh Pal had enjoyed a long, interesting, and fulfilling life, dying an old man: so different to the 'snatching away of a young life' with so much anticipated promise and hope, which described Prince before his sixteenth birthday.*

Tony and Rani's daughters were continuing with their studies and the older girls would finish college this year before university, all so very brave and focused!

How much I missed them all and longed to be with them at this sad time. When that would be possible, no-one knew; only God Himself.

Chapter 2

Looking back - God's Connections

On hearing of Prince's untimely death I had been keen to find someone *special* in India to befriend Tony. In particular I thought that another Indian man would be best, if that were possible.

It happened that I met a lady at our local church in Chineham, Basingstoke, England, whose son lived in Oxford, about 40 miles from there, where he worked as a potter and ceramic artist. He was scheduled to come to Christ Church to give a practical demonstration on how to *throw* a pot, and to talk about his work in general. I was interested in painting porcelain, so went along, hoping to learn as much as I could.

Chatting with Andrew later that day I explained my quest to find someone with a contact in India *'who knew and loved the Lord Jesus'* and would be willing to befriend and help console Tony and his family, at this difficult time. Andrew kindly introduced me to Sunny Sebastian, a friend whom he'd known through visiting an orphanage in South India, where Sunny had been working voluntarily some years before.

Sunny and I communicated via e-mail and agreed that when Peter and I *could* travel to India *we would meet*. Meanwhile Peter and I prayed.

November 2009 India here we come.

We eventually got our air-tickets and headed off to India prior to travelling on to Singapore and Australia intending to visit friends and family.

That meeting was very emotional as Prince had died only a few months before and our hearts cried for Tony and his family. *There were no words that could console.* All we *could* do was show them how much we loved them but most of all pray that God would introduce *Himself* to them in this time of grief and comfort their broken hearts. How much we thanked God that we had been able to make the trip and be there to hold them in our arms

Tony had kindly arranged for Rani's brother Satpal to take us to Chandigarh City, where Sunny and his wife Karin now lived. Sapna (Tony's second daughter) came too.

Chandigarh is a 'City and Union Territory' in the northern region of India and serves as capital city for two states Haryana and Punjab; with what appeared to be quite different cultures. These 'Union Territories' are found throughout all India but are mainly a feature of North India. In Haryana *Hindi* is usually spoken, while in the Punjab, *Punjabi* is the main language used. These languages reflect the predominant *religion in each State*. These are *Hinduism* in the State of Haryana, *Sikhism* in the State of Punjab.

Chandigarh is the first Indian city to have been formerly planned and in contrast to Delhi (the capital city of *all* India) and seemed to me to be much less crowded, with more open spaces and less obvious pollution. Perhaps this is why it's also known as the Garden City.

We remembered with amazement, that it had been nine *long* years since we had *last been* in India, and we could hardly take in how quickly time had flown by and how things had changed.

Stopping off in the city, at a rather up-market restaurant to enjoy a tasty meal, we shared a vegetable curry which was accompanied by the most amazing looking bread. This was conical shaped and puffed up with air, but *"Oh! My!"* it tasted delicious and later I found out it was Poori. In the same restaurant, breads, cakes and sweets were made on the premises and sold to the many business types who stopped for lunch. There was a real buzz all around, the atmosphere feeling more like

London or Paris, so familiar, to us both.

We went to the Zoo and had a fun time with Sapna and a very precious interlude with that sweet young lady. Eventually we went on to a huge lake where lots of families paraded up and down, as might be seen in most European cities. There were babies in plush push-chairs, all looking very chic. Most of the population was dressed in western dress which really surprised me! Surely I thought, *Indian Style* would have been much more practical, cool and beautiful. How very disappointing for me.

The obvious opulence at the lake compared to the sight of those poor families living on the scrap heaps at the edge of the city startled me; so that I felt deeply saddened. I realised in every city there is poverty but here there was such a vast heap of rubbish and so many poverty stricken people living on it. I was deeply moved, as this was totally different to any previous experience of mine.

Then it was 'off' in the car to meet the young couple. Our first meeting with Sunny & Karin was at their apartment block where all the trainee nurses had their own individual accommodation. They had a bright and airy flat and were most welcoming. We stayed less than an hour but *what an amazing and heartwarming time we shared.* As we had conversed frequently *online* prior to our visit, they were fully appraised of Sapna's family loss. Karin and Sapna connected with one another instantly and were soon chatting like old friends. This was such a joy for Peter and me to see, as they exchanged telephone numbers and agreed to keep in touch.

Sunny began to tell us a little of his life story and how he had handed over his life to the Lord Jesus Christ when he was seventeen years old, after a very difficult and unhappy childhood full of poor self-worth at that time! He'd found himself living on the streets, at the age of thirteen!

Eventually, some four or five years later, he had returned home and learnt that Jesus loved him just as he was! He asked God to forgive him and set him free from all the hurt and loss he'd experienced.

He said *"Jesus has totally changed my life and my thinking and given me joy in my heart".*

We could so easily see the beauty of the Saviour reflected in his face as it shone with happiness as he spoke and the obvious peace God had given him. Sunny related his story he mentioned that God had asked him to leave his South Indian roots and come to North India to train as a General Nurse and Midwife.

What a challenge, as here in the North of the country there was a completely different culture and language, not to mention the fact that he would be a mature student!

Wow! Imagine that…

How much he would have to humble himself, having already completed his General Education and Theology Degree and been ordained as a Pastor. This demonstrated clearly to me such a miracle of the grace and the power of God in his life. Proof *if any were needed,* that God always changes us from the inside out, so our attitudes and desires bring glory to Him.

On completion, his wish was to promote *Health, Hygiene and Nutrition* alongside the *Education Project* that he and Karin planned to start in a village, where the Outcast children of Indian Society lived, there in the outskirts of Chandigarh City.

Karin meanwhile related *her* story. When she was just sixteen years old, back in her homeland of Brazil, God had spoken to her in a dream. She said *"God explained that He wanted me to leave home eventually and live in India! There He would lead me to have a School and Social Project for the poor uneducated children in India."*

She told us that she had believed what Jesus told her in her dream and had trained with this in mind.

My heart fairly 'skipped a beat' because God had also laid on my heart this dream of a house where we could have a Social Project, comprising of Education and Health Care for the benefit of the needy children in India!

This was how our dreams united.

The *very first* time Peter and I had gone to visit Tony and his family, in 2000, they had taken us to visit a carpet making factory in the back streets of Karnal City. Here we saw very young children standing on narrow benches reaching high to weave intricate patterns onto huge hanging canvases. These carpets were designed and made to order.

This sight of *endless work* for these little ones had left a *deep impression* on us both, so that, later, when we had seen wonderful new houses being built overlooking Atal

Park in Karnal City, a dream had taken shape and we envisaged a property where we could help those children, in some way, to escape their poverty. This was for us a *pipe dream* as neither of us had the faintest idea *how* it could be realised. *Nevertheless we knew in God's time and will, nothing is impossible.* However, *everyday life* then took over and our dream remained just that.

Now some nine years on, my heart stirred with understanding and hope, as we listened while Sunny and Karin related their dream ... surely *'this'* was God's amazingly great idea!

Both Peter and I felt this incredible closeness of heart and mind with Sunny and Karin and, as I related our mutual *longing to do something practical* for these so precious little ones, we felt united in our purpose. Peter and I made a commitment to do all we could to support this new venture, in prayer, and in whatever way necessary to make those dreams come true in reality, as God would lead us. For we were sure that God's ways are always perfect, beyond, even our wildest dreams, as the bible says:

As for God, his way is perfect: The LORD's word is flawless...
Psalm 18:30 (N.I.V.)

In the meantime, Sunny agreed to get in touch with

Tony and see if he could visit him and his family in Karnal City and also have Tony come to Chandigarh to their home, which was about a two hour journey by car.

Treasured times

Our time with Tony and family flew by all too quickly and so we were on our way once more to Singapore then Australia, before our return to England, *eventually!*

Sunny kept his word and visited Tony at his home telling him about his own life and how much God had done to heal his brokenness and given him a future hope. It appeared that they immediately became really close friends and Tony assured Sunny of a welcome in his home, whenever he could visit.

Chapter 3

Dreams become reality!

Meanwhile Sunny and Karin chatted frequently with us on Skype and we had lots of fun getting to know one another better and talking about the future and where God was leading us.

So in early 2010, *a few months after our visit to India,* they went to the local village and met with the headman's son getting agreement to have the School and Social Work scheme and to visit the families and see how many parents would support and let the children come to the classes. Those who were interested gave details about their circumstances and their children's names, birth-dates (if known) and any other relevant information to enable the teachers to meet their needs.

Sunny rented a garage in the village and Karin did a very professional job preparing the garage as a school room, buying and covering the concrete floor with a large patterned rug, so that they started their classes with everyone sitting on that. She had made some creative posters for the walls and so the s*chool was born!* There were only twelve children none of whom had ever had any lessons previously. Various ages even a little girl of three, who is still at House of Hope, as I write. Punjabi's love to sing and dance, so these subjects were also built into the curriculum and all joined in with great enthusiasm.

Before long there were tables, chairs, books, pencils and a tape recorder for the music, while Karin created fun stories, using a large rag doll. Eventually they managed to provide a daily meal of hot milk and bread for all the children. This was absolutely necessary, as many of these children experienced *days* without any food, their parents working from morning until late at night, leaving their little ones, to fend for themselves, on the streets alone or with older siblings!

Soon Karin had an additional two young teachers, and so the school began to progress. Given this unique opportunity these children grasped it with both hands, being full of interest and keen to learn.

The aim was to teach the lessons in English and Punjabi as well as Hindi (the principal language of India) so that these children could have a wonderful opportunity, to move out of their poverty and become independent in the future, by getting jobs and so providing for themselves and their families.

As Dr Deirdre Shawe, so aptly mentioned, in her foreword to this book, these children were mainly from what is known as the Dalit or Untouchable or Casteless Hindu people. They have little access to any of the privileges which are normal for children in a democratic society. The government clearly states that *all children* are entitled to an education and provides schools accordingly and endeavours to change the circumstances for those children who would be excluded, because of their Caste.

However we learnt that it is widely believed in India that even the *shadow* of a Dalit is corrupted! This could explain why it would appear these families can be treated in any way desired by those of a Higher Caste, which of course is everyone else in that society. Some would even go so far as to say, *"These families are devils!"*

In his interesting and enlightening true life story, entitled 'Death of a Guru', Rabi. R. Maharaj, gives a clear insight into the Hindu Caste System and eastern belief of Karma and the Cycle of Re-incarnation. He says, "Karma states that there can be no forgiveness for mistakes or misdemeanours in the present life. In simple words, how you live in this present life will determine your fate in the next".

According to *Karma* these *Untouchables* or *Casteless* people had not achieved enough *Good Karma* in their previous existence, so now have been *Re-incarnated* as *Casteless* individuals, therefore *Outcasts* from society. Being their own fault and resulting fate allows for a lack of any real sympathy for their present position. Their suffering, seen *as necessary,* for them to return in their next *Re-Incarnation,* (if possible) in a caste because of their better or *Good Karma*.

Later I would see this philosophy in practice for myself, when I witnessed little children begging on the street in front of the designer shops in Sector 17 of Chandigarh City. The door attendants chasing them away like rabid dogs, with kicks, shouts and stones.

A belief like this would have caused me to despair except that I had met the Risen Christ and knew through my personal relationship with Him, *that no one believing and trusting Jesus need be afraid either of death or the afterlife. Jesus, God's own Son, had become my perfect sinless substitute, taking all my sins and nailing them to His cross, by His sacrifice I am forgiven by believing in His Name.*

I have found I don't have to try harder I just need to lean harder on my all sufficient Redeemer and Lord. How very thankful I am that He died so that I could live, and now He lives forever glorified and sitting at God's right hand in Heaven. Victorious over death and sin! The Bible tells us clearly in its last book ... 'Revelation'.

When I die or Jesus returns to take me, I will be where He is forever. Such incredible love and provision! And even more amazing and wonderful it is to know, that it is of no consequence, where or into which family I have been born.(How wonderful is that truth to me)

For the Bible assures me:

God so greatly loved and dearly prized the world that He [even] gave up His only begotten (unique) Son, so that whoever believes in (trusts in, clings to, relies on) Him shall not perish (come to destruction, be lost) but have eternal (everlasting) life. John 3:v16 Amp Bible

When the Messiah was executed on the stake as a criminal, I was too; so that my proud ego no longer lives. But the Messiah lives in me, and the life I now live in my body I live by the same trusting faithfulness that the Son of God had, who loved me and gave himself up for me. Galatians 2:20 (CJB)

In the Bible it also states;

It is appointed for men to die once, but after this the judgment. (ERV.- AleR.)

Jesus said, "Let not your hearts be troubled. Believe in God believe also in me. In my Father's house are many rooms. If it were not true, would I have told you that I go to prepare a place for you? And if I go and prepare a place for you, I will come again and will take you to myself, that where I am you may be also. John 14: 1-3 (ESV)

Sometime later I wrote the poem at the beginning of this book, to express what God had shown me about this freedom in Jesus.

Chapter 4

Changing Times

Education is compulsory in India for all children as I have stated and expected in any democratic country. However the reality is that in most of these villages children must be sent to work, as without their earnings, families cannot afford to eat! Education would be the last thing on their agenda, *I imagined.*

Free education, on the other hand, could enable them to understand how to keep themselves healthy and clean and teach them the three R's, as we say, (Reading, Writing, and Arithmetic) which are essential for progress in modern society. Without this opportunity their future would remain bleak and *without someone to care, surely these little children's lives would be a copy of their unfortunate parentage.*

Our overriding aim, at the school in Chandigarh, was and is to teach them how to become good Indian citizens, where their changed lives could eventually bring freedom to others born in the same situation, giving them the impetus to move from poverty to reasonable and fruitful lives. Teaching moral values based on Christian principals such as cleanliness, truthfulness, honesty, integrity and love for one's neighbour as one's self, a work ethic and appreciation of their own self worth, together with a basic education, would prepare them to become part of the New India, (as they themselves talk about so frequently, with such hope and enthusiasm) where all could be free. They could then reach their own potential, reducing the ability of cruel taskmasters to exploit them for their own ends.

Heart wrenching news!

2010, later the same year that the school had opened in India, *back home in England* our youngest son's wife Nicola (our precious daughter-in–law) was diagnosed with breast cancer. We were devastated! I was soon *fully involved* with Graham and Nicola's two little girls, Jessica aged 7 and Mia just 4 years old.

Soon my days would be full, taking and collecting them from school and nursery whenever needed. Spending time with the girls was one of the most rewarding, satisfying and delightful times in my life but also *very tiring*. I was surprised how much energy it took and would come home and *collapse in a heap* until Peter came back from work; and *I thought I was fit!*

Nicky (as she likes to be called) on the other hand was coping remarkably well and, as ever, was never miserable in spite of all the horrid treatments she had to endure. It was during this harrowing time that I started to write poetry. I found this an incredible way of relieving my mind of pain, laying it before God in prayer and finding the solace that only He could give. I also found God giving me *words* which I prayerfully hoped would enable *healing of minds* for others in similar circumstances.

Meanwhile we also had the joy of babysitting our little grandson Morgan when necessary. He is our eldest son Paul's child, being about the same age as Jessica, Graham's eldest. Morgan was born on March 17th (St. Patrick's Day) while Jessica's birthday is 8th May, both in 2002. Mia was an October baby born three years later in 2006. Certainly they were and remain the greatest joy of both our lives.

In November of that year we had eagerly anticipated a trip to Queensland in Australia planning to visit family. My brother David and his wife Dee had planned to come with us. They had never been to Australia so we'd made a decision to fly out there and then cruise home.

However we got a call from David to say *he* had cancer

of the bladder and would have to stay at home to have an operation followed by other treatment and had no idea how long all that would take.

Naturally we reconsidered the trip. Praying fervently for his speedy recovery and strength for whatever lay ahead. We both managed to get to Northern Ireland before he went in for surgery and found him calm having a strong faith and belief that God would meet his every need whatever the future held.

Now that Australia was *off the agenda* that Christmas we would try to get to India instead. Peter and I both had a deep desire to see the new school and meet the children there and Sunny and Karin too. A visit with Tony and family was also anticipated. However flights were difficult to arrange at short notice and with lengthy waiting times in Delhi Airport before onward travel to Chandigarh City itself.

Instead of travelling we decided to spend our Christmas and New Year with the grand- children in England, and had a fun and festive holiday season. Soon Peter was back to work having used up all his leave until summer. *Now,* if I went to India this would mean me travelling alone again, as I did 1999, not something I relished…however with a six month visa still available to me, we continued to check flight dates.

Once again we would wait on the Lord and continue to pray for God's plan to be revealed.

Tony and Family

During this time I had some difficulty once again contacting Tony and family and had learned from Rajeev and Vishakha (Tony's niece and husband) that Tony was still struggling with the heart breaking loss of his only son. Added to this agony, Rani, his wife, had continued to be very ill! My heart felt overwhelmed with sadness for them both and the obvious pain the whole family were enduring. *When could I reasonably go back to India? What could I do?*

Unexpectedly we had the most exciting news from Sunny and Karin, they were expecting their *first* baby the following year in March 2011. *Now more than ever we longed to get to India, once more.*

Wonderful and heartwarming news, David was fully recovered from his illness, how very happy we were.

Chapter 5

Chandigarh Welcomes

Early one morning in February the New Year of 2011 Peter suddenly said to me "*I think you should go to India now"* I jumped at the chance, as we were still feeling a deep concern for Tony and his family. Searching the web we found a flight with only two and a half hours wait in Delhi Airport and we felt at peace about that, this time.

I arrived in Chandigarh City Airport after an excellent and uneventful flight, Sunny met me as agreed and I felt most welcomed to their home. This special time with both of them was like a little touch of *heaven on earth*, as we prayed, chatted and laughed together. This was now March 2011 and Karin's first baby was due on the 16th day of the month while my flight home was scheduled for the fourteenth day. I felt quite confident, thinking that the baby would not arrive before the due date (as it was their first baby) so just relaxed and enjoyed this precious time together.

We wandered around the city and also Sector 17 where we marveled at the expensive designer shops and the wonderful restaurants. However the best treat of all was those *home-made dishes* cooked by Karin, that we shared. Absolutely scrumptious! Hours and hours of companionable conversation filled our days too, getting to know one another better, until we felt like true family! *Surely this was a gift from God to us all.* While we anticipated Karin's new baby and the arrival of Karin's sister from Brazil, Sunny took me to visit the hospital where he was training, in a place called Mohali. Here I met some of the staff including those caring for Karin at the ante-natal clinic and had a most interesting time.

My Family in Karnal

Some days later I went to see Tony and family on their farm in Karnal and had a time of *joy and sadness* with them. Rani had to go to hospital as she had gallstones which were agony. She was given some pain relief and instructed to return for removal or dispersal of the stones, as soon as she was strong enough to do so. I was very relieved that her pain had abated and she was able to rest at home and converse more easily.

However I had been greatly shocked to see how thin Tony David (my adopted son) had become and I could see that he still had a problem with drinking alcohol to excess. We had the opportunity to chat alone, on the flat roof of his house, and he asked me to pray for him as he felt very lonely. He also said he thought that this time my visit, would be the catalyst which would, with God's help, enable him to beat the drink and start to live again! I fervently prayed that this would be so, as I put my arms around him praying for God's strength to meet his need.

Tony took me to see the government-run school where he taught, in the local village. *Here* it was easy to see how much he loved teaching the children and especially these less advantaged little ones. I'd known he was well educated, having sufficient qualifications to actually tutor the teachers, never mind the children! Now I saw this in practice, as he shared with me how often he was able to give guidance and help to his colleagues who would come to ask him for advice. It was obvious to me that *all* including the Principal of the school held Tony in high regard. They were all most welcoming and took time out of their busy schedule to talk with me and give an overview of their school ethos and plans for the future. I appreciated their kindness more than I could say.

Tony also showed a positive interest in our little School and Social Health Project at its inception, promising to use his skills advising and supporting Sunny, Karin and myself where possible.

To this end he agreed to come on the Sunday before I returned home, to talk it through with Sunny *man to man*.

One of the joys of being there at the farm, (their home) was meeting my old friend of a lifetime Pal (Tony's father) and although concerned for the current state of affairs in his family, he expressed his pleasure in seeing me again and being able to chat to someone from his heart. I promised again to pray for them all. We had a long walk and I truly hadn't then realised that he was in his eightieth year. He was still so remarkably sprightly, walking fast and assuredly with his usual military stance.

Even so, *for some unknown reason*, as I left their home, I had a strong sense that this could be our last meeting. *As it turned out, that was the case as he died eleven months later, in February, the following year.*

Now looking back, I have no regrets and feel sure God took me there at that difficult time to be a friend to Pal and enable him to share his concerns. God had been so gracious to allow us that friendly time and last farewell in peace.

Tony *did come* as promised on the Sunday and we all shared a wonderful meal in a delightful Indian Restaurant near Sunny's home. These *two sons of my heart* conversed and planned together about the School Project. Tony knew quite a lot as he was responsible for the administration at the village school he taught in, while Sunny had made enquiries about legalities in his State of Punjab and had liaised with the Village headman there.

To my joy, there seemed to be a virtual meeting of minds! Sunny prayed for us all including, Shanti (Tony's sister) and Sapna (Tony's second daughter). I too added my prayers as requested, for blessings *to be poured out* on the whole family and the peace of *Jesus Christ God's own Son* to be made real to them.

I had the special joy of seeing Sunny and Karin's new baby girl before I left for home in England. She was born when I was in Karnal at Tony's home! Karin's sister Cintia had arrived safely from Brazil the day previously so was there with Karin for the birth. Wow! How's that for good timing.

God does all things well. How very thankful I was to Him for allowing me to be there at that special time.

Chapter 6

House of Hope Project 2012

The initial school was started two years previously in 2010, in a village on the outskirts of *Chandigarh City*, where these disadvantaged children and their families lived.

Sometime after (Peter and my) first visit to India (in 2000) we had seen a television programme set in Uttar Pradesh (described as the poorest state in all India) where families were living in huge cracked sewer pipes which had been left over from building projects. These pipes became extremely cold and wet in the monsoon season and unbearably hot in the height of summer! So many of these residents, when they were offered the opportunity of a loan from prospective employers to fund the journey to the State of Punjab, and a promise of jobs and better living conditions, had grasped the chance to better their lives. The reality turned out to be very different to their dream, as many now continued to work on the scrap heaps collecting plastic for others to re-cycle and sell, but with the additional problem that they were in debt to their employers for their fare from state to state. Little had they understood that in a very short time the cost of that loan had tripled with interest owed and the wages paid were never likely to make a dent in the overall debt! They would never be able to repay their employers, so were in effect now slave labour.

Most worked from early morning until late at night doing these menial tasks including cleaning the public latrines. There was no thought or provision for health and hygiene or safety, as they worked in bare feet with rags for clothes and as soon as their children were walking, they too, would be working with their parents in these dangerous environments. This would then mean that *as the norm* the children would often go all day without any food and certainly education was not possible for them. Return to their home state was clearly impossible.

Our prayer was that House of Hope School and Health programme could in some small way change lives for the better, for families like these. Especially, we anticipated that their children having access to free education would give them the choice to make their own decisions for their future. Giving opportunities to become doctors, nurses, teachers, engineers, business owners or whatever they would choose in life.

Health education would teach the parents to care more

adequately for themselves and their children and maintain better hygiene standards preventing disease and illness.

Two years on, the School and Health Project was progressing well with numbers increasing daily and children and families becoming more and more enthusiastic as they witnessed their children's progress and learned a better way of life in general.

During summer months the temperatures can rise to as high as plus fifty degrees centigrade, so much of the unnecessary work is abandoned until the weather cools, with the wealthy families going on holiday to the lower *Himalayan cities to* stay cool and sending their employees back to their former homes as their employers decided.

Sunny, Karin and Deborah were very much in need of a well earned change and chance to visit friends and family by now. A trip to Singapore and Kerala in the South of India was a lovely time of refreshing for them all and they had a fabulous time.

Progress

As the numbers of children grew there was a lack of sufficient space in the garage and with no individual rooms for different age groups the situation became untenable. There was an urgent need for Sunny and Karin to look for an alternative venue where the House of Hope could be allowed to grow without these restrictions. This in itself presented many difficulties, not least culturally, as many residents and property owners in the area would not tolerate these Dalit children accessing their premises or being within reach.

Nevertheless we all believed that God's ways are perfect and *nothing* is ever too hard for Him.

The owners of the garage premises were reluctant to see the school move away. They had been very pleased with the standards of care and cleanliness observed there. Sunny and Karin had made every effort to teach the children social skills, by taking them to their *own* home for showers and food, and also to the local market where they learnt about the different foods and the benefits of good nutrition.

However, the need for space, flexibility and expansion was paramount. So *the search was on* for a suitable building in an area where these children could feel safe from hostility and still be within their home locality.

A new property was being built in the vicinity of the village. Sunny approached the owner and negotiated rental of the whole building on completion. This would be available early in July that year. Wow! We were so excited at this miracle of grace.

In the meantime, *before the new term* started and on Sunny and Karin's return from their holiday in Singapore, two of the older pupils Ganga and Arjun, needed to be transferred to a secondary school, both being eleven years old and having reached the required standard of education to enter the government school locally. This was surely an amazing achievement for all involved, as these boys had no previous education whatsoever.

Now, how to get them accepted was the big question? They had no birth certificates or identity papers, so Sunny set about acquiring affidavits for them and negotiating places for them in the local government school. After a lot of work and effort he achieved his aim and got them admission! Everyone was excited to see them go to the senior school and their parents were also delighted with their ongoing progress.

These two boys came every evening to Sunny and Karin's home for extra tuition, to enable them to keep up with their class mates. Sunny monitored these children's studies and ensured they were treated well at the new school. Ganga had said that he wanted to become a doctor but Arjun had not then decided his future. Both were very keen to learn. I remember them well from my visit in 2011 in the original school building.

New School Building

Joy of Joys, Sunny and Karin rang to say the new school building was completed and would be ready for them to move into by July 2012. This was a house of three stories, set out in three individual flats, which meant each floor had its own shower room and kitchen plus three reasonably sized rooms which could be used as classrooms. *What could be better? God does all things with excellence. How we thanked Him.*

Now it would be possible to have separate rooms and also teach basic Health and Hygiene in a very practical way as they could shower on arrival at the school, comb their hair, clean their teeth etc.

It hadn't been possible to provide a proper meal for all sixty children previously and this had been one of our urgent prayers, when an Indian couple who owned a language school nearby, offered to cover this cost for the foreseeable future, how wonderfully generous. We sang praise to God.

Teachers

Two lady teachers came to this new school with Das, (Sunny's brother) who had stayed to help after his motor bike accident having broken some bones in his foot preventing him from returning to his work at Y.W.A.M., (youth with a mission).

Both of these girls had taught in the old school previously but had moved away from that area when they got married. One of them Vishakha, had experience working in various social work projects throughout India and pledged herself now to work again with Karin and Sunny to fulfil the dream for the House of Hope, for as long as possible.

All of these teachers spoke fluently each of the languages needed for understanding and progress. This also meant they were able to build rapport with the children's parents and local people within the village community.

Lessons were divided into morning and afternoon sessions with around thirty children in each. Younger children were taught before lunch and older children later in the day. With the extra space it was now possible to start a teaching programme of craftwork, for the parents in particular. Sewing skills were a priority so that the families could start their own home industries and become more self-reliant and financially secure. Independently they would be able to sell their creations and help begin work towards a better life.

It might even be possible to employ one or two of these parents doing practical jobs in the House of Hope and so create an opening for other possibilities in the future.

Now Sunny and Karin felt there was a need to have *house parents* who would be able to live *on site* to secure the building and do any maintenance that might be necessary while participating in support of the children.

Vishakha and her husband Satzin volunteered for this position and soon they created a more homely atmosphere for these young people, even though this was still a day school.

We were so grateful to God for Sunny and Karin's commitment and love for these children, shown by them in many different ways. We continue also to be very thankful for all our friends and family who pray daily for everyone there, especially that the children and parents will be protected and blessed.

How time had flown by.

It was now 2013, where had the time gone, we

wondered happily? How quickly time flies! Deborah was now two years old and full of life and laughter. It was always so exciting to see her online and hear her sing and chat in English. She was a really happy and cute little girl! She was a real joy for everyone.

After his Singapore trip (during the summer of 2012) it was *back to work* for Sunny as his final nursing examinations loomed in December of that year. Karin meanwhile had also started studying the Montessori method of teaching, online, and was progressing well. She felt this qualification would be beneficial for her to help the children to gain understanding more easily and speed up their learning.

It continually filled me with amazement, as to how they had realised all these *many achievements*: further teacher training; nursing training, while bringing up their own daughter; as meanwhile everything was progressing rapidly with the School. Out of these amazing sixty children, eight more eleven year olds had been enrolled in the mainstream secondary Schools. The dream was certainly more of a reality than any of us could ever have envisaged.

In the evenings the children from the senior school continued to come for an hour of tuition with Sunny and Karin keeping them in touch while advancing their learning.

On Fridays a *Children's Club* had been started, since coming to the new School building and this continued to be a time of excitement and relaxation for all the children, who joined in with enthusiasm. They played outdoor games, board games, had music with songs and dancing or watched films. All this was something these young people *never* before had an opportunity to participate in. They were so much in need of fun and laughter, for even a short period of time in their busy and difficult lives. How my heart sang with joy to see their smiling faces, such a change from those sad, lonely and frightened looks displayed so clearly, when first I met them in 2011 at the very start of the project.

Chapter 7

Great achievements

2013 Sunny's graduation as a Registered General Nurse and Midwife, followed by a six month internship completed his training course. This was a great achievement! After completing his charge nurse induction he even managed a Critical Illness nursing course. He achieved all this without complaint and had also found favour with his colleagues, senior staff, and patients.

Peter and I were delighted to see all this happening and the rapid progression of the School project at the same time.

Children and Teachers

Many more families had requested to join the School, but the need for more staff restricted entry for the time being. Karin was still the principal teacher, preparing the curriculum with the teachers every week and overseeing the project. Sunny and Karin held *teacher tuition classes* weekly and planned the weeks ahead with their staff.

The teaching continued with classes in Reading, Writing, Art, Music, Drama, Computer Studies, Health, Hygiene, Nutrition and History. It was comprehensive and beneficial for the children's future.

Yet another six boys had achieved learning to a standard to qualify them to enter the next grade School too and all proved successful in their studies! Their progress continued to be monitored regularly by Sunny with their teachers, and ongoing visits by him to see that they continued to be accepted socially. All these young teenagers came each evening to House of Hope for extra tuition, keeping in touch with House of Hope, and their friends there. This was even more important now that they were teenagers! They also loved the Children's club on Fridays, and it continued to be a roaring success of fun and laughter for all.

Vishakha and Satzin had proved to be excellent *House Parents* creating the needed stability and safety for the children and the premises.

In the mean time some dear friends from Christ Church, Basingstoke, had not forgotten the House of Hope either and had arranged a most exciting *curry dinner* held at there, to update everyone about the school. This was so successful that a message on Face book, posted by Gordon Randall, said *"Sorry no more seats available"*.

"Well done", Shubnum Gill and friends who worked so hard to make it a brilliant evening. Peter and I were only sorry not to have been there to taste all that delicious food.

Every day we give thanks to our Majestic God for all the love and generosity shown by those dear friends throughout the world who continue faithfully to make the Hope Project a victory for these little children and their families. We finished that year with grateful thanks and a song in our hearts for all God's continued grace and provision.

Chapter 8

New Life style for us!

At the beginning of 2014, Peter and I had been resident in Majorca, Balearic Isles, Spain, for more than a year and were greatly blessed with much better health and many lovely new friends. Naturally we were thrilled that all family and many friends came to visit us regularly and we had quality time and fun with them all. Our calendar was fully booked for that whole year from early spring, so there was no chance we'd be lonely or bored.

It was a particular joy for us to spend more time with our precious grandchildren and family who really enjoy holidays here. For the *'hale and hearty'* there is lots to do and see, with the sea, beach, harbour, sailing, fishing, surfing, mountain climbing and cycling, to name but a few outdoor pursuits. Walking around the harbour and marina and stopping off at the many coffee shops for delicious drinks and cakes is our greatest pleasure!

Peter *works that off* with a swim in our communal swimming pool, when he's in the mood, while I relax happily watching him and reading a book. Often just sitting in front of the harbour side watching all the boats sailing in and out I find fascinating and delightful too.

Since coming to live in Spain, Tony and family have continued to keep in touch with us! We thank God from the bottom of our hearts as Tony is now fully healed in mind and body a 'miracle of grace'. He is teaching and involved with his cousin in running their political campaigns to promote better conditions for all the citizens of India. I thank God everyday for His incredible love to me and for the healing of my precious son.

His older daughters, Meenakshi and Sapna studying hard in their final year at University, having completed their examinations to this level, both aiming to be engineers and working towards their Bachelor of Science Degrees while the younger girls, Pooja and Fairy commenced college in the September semester 2014. We are delighted to hear of their continued success.

Although Tony had struggled emotionally and physically, he had never once left his family without the future they needed, in education and culture. Private education for four girls is a huge commitment financially (as many of you will know) combined with the ongoing surgery and treatment Rani has needed and the responsibility for family weddings Tony has had, in the extended family, certainly created a big expense!

However, Tony has met all these challenges head on. I have no doubt *his pocket is somewhat lighter* (as he would say) nevertheless Peter and I are immensely proud of him and we love the whole family dearly.

Thanking too, our Mighty and Victorious God who does all things superbly. He has been faithful in providing for us here in a *new country* and we have found the transition remarkably easy with His help. To see my husband so much fitter brings the greatest happiness to my heart. We celebrated twenty-five years of marriage last year and feel ready for another twenty-five!

Chapter 9

Change is Inevitable!

2014 has certainly proved to be year of c*hange* at the House of Hope. Sunny's brother Das had left the school (as planned) and returned to South India where he met and married a beautiful lady. We wished them both a *blessed marriage* and long life together. The House parent couple, Vishakha & Satzin had also moved on to new horizons and again we wished them all the best for their future.

The children who had been at the House of Hope from the beginning were now ready or would be ready soon, to move up to the secondary schools by the summer vacation. *What success!* Praise our God and thanks to Sunny and Karin and their team. *Although very exciting* this would be a *major undertaking* involving finding schools to suit all their needs, and of course, continuing to follow their progress. *What a mammoth task!*

Similarly the other teenage children, already placed, would need continued support, with evening tutorials as before! Therefore with this in mind, Sunny had taken a *major decision* to stop nursing for the present and concentrate fully on these children and their families rather than taking more new students.

Furthermore, Sunny and Karin would soon need to take a much needed sabbatical year, having been committed whole heartedly to the House of Hope, without wavering since its inception in March 2010. This would ideally commence October 2014.

What of House of Hope? How should we proceed until Sunny and Karin's return? Who would or could fill the gap? Both they and we, and many *faithful friends* were praying to know how to proceed in the best way possible, looking to see what God had in store for their future…

Once more we would pray for God's guidance, which always produced the best results. For His timing is *'Perfect' we fully believed and had proved so many times in the past.*

Psalm 18 assures us of this:

As for God, His way is perfect! The word of the Lord is tested *and* tried; He is a shield to all those who take refuge *and* put their trust in Him. Psalm 18:30 (AMP Bible)

Chapter 10

Where do we go from here?

This was a major question and we had been presented with lots of new and exciting possibilities.

Way back in 2012, before we'd even considered retiring to live in Majorca, our dear friends Phillip and Elizabeth Shannon, whom I'd known for years through our mutual friends Ted and Lily Frampton and S.A.S.R.A. (Soldier's Airmen's Scripture Readers Association) generously offered us free tickets to the Chelsea Flower Show and *even provided an extra two* for my cousin Ken Forsythe and his wife Milda, to join us on the day. How amazingly generous and we enjoyed a fabulous day.

Phillip had taken over charge of the *Chelsea Pensioners Hospital* after finishing his military service in the Irish Guards where he had been an accomplished *Band Master Major*.

On that day, I had been introduced briefly to Dr. Deirdre Shawe, a *Specialist Rheumatologist* who worked at our local hospital in Basingstoke, although her home was nearer to London. I'd given her my contact details and invited her to stay over at our home if ever she was working very late and needed a bed. I also gave her the link to my book .Sometime later, she contacted me to say she was going abroad to a medical conference and would be in touch on her return, and had ordered the book.

We were both busy with our lives and so time passed! Then to my surprise and pleasure Deirdre rang up to say she had unearthed my telephone number and had read the book. She was keen to meet and chat about it with me.

Wow! How very strange and exciting as Peter and I were packed up and leaving for Spain the very next week! (April 2013)

Happily we arranged to meet for dinner at the local Chinese restaurant and catch up. This was a most enjoyable and profitable evening.

Deirdre was enthusiastic about the House of Hope Project and interested to get involved. Meantime we would both pray and keep in touch. When we were settled in our new home *then* we would discuss the possibilities together. I am convinced God never makes mistakes no matter how long it takes and His appointments are *Divine Appointments* with purpose.

So through Skype and email we kept our budding friendship and eventually I was able to introduce her to Sunny and Karin whom she contacted directly.

Peter and I had arrived here in Majorca at the end of April 2013 and now, almost a year later, Deirdre informed me that she was going to Pakistan to a former colleague's hospital to give some lectures in rheumatology.

"*Oh! My!*" I thought, *so near to India, I wonder if there is any possibility of her visiting House of Hope?, a pipe dream surely!*" To our amazement and delight she told us she also had this idea. *Was there any chance?* Her time was very limited; could she get a flight to Delhi and then what about another connecting flight on to Chandigarh City, the chances, slim indeed.

Sunny and Karin were ecstatic at the prospect, having become quite friendly with her, through Skype themselves. Yet again it was a *wait on God's time* and if it was in His plan all would work out without a hitch I truly believed. *Oh, what joy I felt, I could hardly take it in...* The flights were booked, visa received and she was ready for the *off,* how we shouted "*Halleluiah!*" This was such an answer to our prayers for the project, as we had all along felt there needed to be some dedicated Health and Welfare input, as part of the gift to these families.

Sunny had become a trained 'General Nurse and Midwife' so in my mind this was *surely* part of the plan.

My God will liberally supply (fill to the full) your every need according to His riches in glory in Christ Jesus. Philippians 4:19 (AMP) Bible

The time came for this unprecedented visit just about one year on from the time we had discussed House of Hope while enjoying that lovely meal at 'Am' Restaurant in Basingstoke.

Deirdre surely came at the perfect time

She and Sunny went to visit the homes of the parents and children of those who were present or past pupils of the House of Hope School to tell them that they were setting up a Health clinic the next day, and invited anyone interested to attend. As ever the Indian families went to great lengths to be hospitable having bought some snacks *to give to them* during their visit to their homes, *even though many would have nothing left for themselves to eat,* we were sure! These homes in the *slum area* consist of one dark room with perhaps up to six people living there! However Deirdre noted they had made excellent use of the limited space and endeavoured to keep the area as clean and tidy as possible, but without adequate water supply, electricity and sanitary provision, this is especially difficult if not near impossible for our western minds to conceive!

I reflected…belief in Karma and the cycle of re-incarnation, now accepted by so many people in Western society, makes the caste system possible, leaving these poor families without any future hope.

I thanked God so often that *'I had been set free by my belief in the blood of Jesus and have no fear or need to try to take a chance on my future. Jesus has done it all on the Cross when He died and took my sins on His sinless self; conquered 'Death and Sin' and now sits at God's right hand in Heaven, 'giving me His life in exchange for mine'.*

This I know to be true, as daily God lives in me by the power of His 'Holy Spirit'. I am not perfect and never shall be in this world, but my 'God alone is Perfect'.

The song says: *'Amazing Grace How sweet the sound, He saved a wretch like me'* written by John Newton between 1760 -1770.

I have been 'Twice Born' once as a baby and secondly by the 'Holy Spirit's' power when I asked God for forgiveness and accepted Jesus as Redeemer and Lord, I don't have to fear the next cycle of re-incarnation and whatever I might return as, if not perfectly united with God.

I think deep down in our hearts we know that could never be a reality because none of us is ever likely to live a completely sinless life...

Jesus said to Nicodemus the High Religious leader of his day...

"You must be 'Born Again' not of the flesh but of the Spirit I assure you, most solemnly I tell you, that unless a person is born again (anew, from above), he cannot ever see (know, be acquainted with, and experience) the kingdom of God". John 3: 3 (AMP) Bible

It's no longer what I have to do for God but all about what He has already done for me. Thank God, how liberating that truly is!

On the following day, Deirdre with Sunny's help purchased all the equipment needed to hold the Health clinic. All three, Deirdre, Sunny, Karin and *of course we mustn't forget Deborah*, set up the room ready for an evening session. The clinic was a resounding success. All those who attended were assessed for signs of malnutrition, and also underwent eye, throat, heart, lung and spinal examination, together with a blood pressure check. Two individuals were referred to the local hospital for further investigation of problems identified.

These families told Sunny and Karin they had been very moved by this experience as they had *never ever* had a doctor or nurse touch them before or take any interest in their welfare! If they had managed to get the funds together to go to the doctor he would simply give them some tablets and take their money. *They had no idea what the medication was and as for side effects, no advice.*

I could understand some of the 'mind set' that made this possible among people who otherwise were often very caring, as I began to understand more fully their religious and cultural background, but for me it was absolutely Satan's big deceptive lie! How cruel is the evil one. Thank God for Jesus!

Deirdre said she felt very blessed to be there and meet with Sunny and Karin. She was astonished at all they had achieved in such a few short years. In a couple of days she herself had achieved incredible and life changing acts of love. We are so thankful to her and know this is only the beginning of something bigger.

Chapter 11

Deirdre tells her Story.

Deirdre related her story to me in this way.

I went to a Christian youth group when I was around 16 years old and found a faith in God...but did not understand the Cross or who Jesus was.

Subsequently I went to medical school in London, and soon after qualifying as a doctor I met Mike, as we were working at the same hospital in Plymouth, Devon. We married four years later...and then had five children, including twins, in the space of six and a half years!

Gradually I lost what faith I had...*but always knew I would need to turn around and face God one day.*

Mike decided to train in Emergency Medicine and, after a variety of different hospital jobs and a year in general practice, I decided to pursue a hospital-based career in Rheumatology. I was fortunate to be able to work part-time which made it possible to spend time with the children as well as keeping a career going.

Tragedy struck

When a close friend died of cancer, I decided to try going to church again, but by the time I got there, with 5 children in tow, and got them settled...it was time to go home! I got disheartened and stopped going.

About 8 years later in 2004, my second child went to hear a Christian band play at a concert and became a Christian on the spot! When she told me, I suggested she went to the church I had tried previously...she did this and then took her elder brother with her. This resulted in him getting converted over a longer period of time. They later took one of my twins with them, and she got converted too!

I started going to church with them in 2007, and was immediately "knocked sideways" by the gospel, as explained by the minister of the church, who was a brilliant preacher.

I decided to look into things further and went to a 'Christianity Explored' course, where I felt like 'a fish out of water' at first.

I had spent so many years bringing up children or working in hospital that it was hard to talk about myself or what I might believe. In fact I nearly left after the third week, but thankfully a fascination for the gospel kept me there!

We studied the book of Mark, the second Gospel in the New Testament of the Holy Bible.

Several weeks after the course finished, I was working on the computer late at night and saw an image of Jesus, walking across in front of me saying "Follow me".

I knew immediately that this was what I wanted to do, even though I did not realise what it would mean. Just prior to this I had got to the point where I wanted to believe but couldn't. There was a gap I could not leap across, but when I looked behind, the gap was even bigger...so I couldn't go back.

Somehow, after I had seen the image of Jesus, I found myself on the other side, having leapt the gap of faith without knowing how it had happened! …

My knowledge of Deirdre is of a very stable individual, not given to any hysteria or dramatics so I asked her: "Deirdre how did you know for sure that it was Jesus you saw"? She simply said "I don't know how I knew - I just knew"…

It seemed to me a bit like 'falling in love' as you just know but you can't explain how you know! This brought to my mind the verse in the Holy Bible where Jesus said…

Behold, I stand at the door and knock; if anyone hears and

listens to and heeds My voice and opens the door, I will come in to him and will eat with him, and he [will eat] with Me.
Revelation 3:20 (Amp) Bible

'What an amazing banquet ready for all who open that door!'

So, although I have never seen Jesus for myself I know Him too, in my heart; because I have proved I can trust Him completely, as over the years He continues to change me from the inside out. God certainly has a wonderful plan for all of our lives and that being true in Deirdre's life too.

I was overwhelmed with thankfulness for her love and commitment to these little children in India. She said she needed to go there to understand fully the situation and appreciate the need. I fully concur with this and hope to encourage others to come out and become involved. We're sure no one will ever be the same again.

How tremendous; and this is only the beginning!

Deirdre has many great ideas to move the health side of the 'project' forward and has even taken an updated course in Infectious Diseases and Nutrition for the Third World.

She has plans for training a 'Health Care Worker' who would work in the School and village. She has procured this training through a well known charity, run by qualified doctors who will allow the House of Hope to join their own health trainees, with additional update or refresher courses available at intervals.

Planning herself to visit at least once a year, she has approached friends and colleagues who may also be interested to be part of this new exciting venture.

Already in the few months since her visit she has worked tirelessly to find suitable contacts and interested parties to improve House of Hope's future. Praise our Risen Lord. Soon she would give personal updates to any group wishing to learn more first hand.

Chapter 12

Friends of 'House of Hope'

At Christmas the House of Hope Children created lovely handmade cards for our friends with their names and photographs on them. They were simply beautiful.

We have plans to start a *'Pen Pal'* connection between these friends and the children so that they can write to those who are interested and bring them up to date with their progress. It will also be an opportunity for the children to improve their 'Language' skills. Maybe even chat together on Skype, creating a closer bond between them. So again these are possibilities which we're sure will come to fruition.

Moving on 2014

How pleased we were to hear from Sunny and Karin that *all* the children from House of Hope School have reached the required standard that summer term (as anticipated) and so were able to integrate into the mainstream senior school. *Well done everyone.*

Sunny had negotiated and enrolled all the children en-mass into the local school (a miracle in itself) with agreement to take other children when they reach this level in the future.

I looked on with astonishment and gratitude remembering how difficult it had been at the beginning to get *even one* of these 'Dalit' children into any mainstream school, never mind one where there is proper teaching and care for the pupils. Now it was possible for Sunny and Karin, to effectively manage the evening tuition for the more senior children and maintain their progress. They had also moved into the school building, to live there temporarily until other house parents were appointed. This worked well, making ongoing contact with the families easier on a day to day basis.

Deborah said one day (shortly after their move) *"I don't want to go back to that other house I want to live here"*. We felt so happy for the whole family.

Pastures new!

At last, the time had come for Sunny and Karin's sabbatical year. After so long, without stopping for any significant length of time, they really needed this break. We were so delighted that this opportunity for them to have a real rest and change of scenery had become a reality. However Sunny, Karin and ourselves, from a purely human prospective, were somewhat apprehensive about their replacement.

It would be essential to have someone take over who would not only be capable but most of all would have a true heart for the 'children's welfare and future. The time was drawing nearer with lots of possible offers of help but we had to wait God's choice or it certainly wouldn't work out.

Deep in my heart I knew it to be true that *'Jesus is faithful who promised, He also will do it'*.

He is a rock. What he does is perfect. All his ways are fair.
He is a faithful God, who does no wrong. He is honourable
and reliable. Deuteronomy 32:4 (GW) Bible

So we prayed believing for not just good but the best. I always think there is good or there is the best: God always goes for the best when we *believe and leave the choices to Him*.

However the waiting tests our faith!

I had learnt about 'Faith in God's Provision' from my mother but I realised one could never live through someone else's experience; we must always prove it in our own lives.

Sunny and family were due to travel to Kerala South India (Sunny's parents home) at the end of July and as it was already early Spring, *time was of the essence!* Of course they were actively looking for the right replacements.

Such excitement!

Sunny informed us that two young men, Benjamin and Joseph, who worked in an orphanage in South India felt God was asking them to go to Chandigarh in North India. They had trained with YWAM (Youth with a Mission) previously. Both were leaders. This connection had come about because Sunny had some twenty years before volunteered at an orphanage in Goa, South India and knew these boys, but I'll tell that story later…

Was this God's Plan?

Sunny agreed to have them come and see and work at the House of Hope for a month, so they could all be sure this was God's place for them and House of Hope. During the first two weeks Sunny and Karin would be able to see their hearts and decide whether they were suitable and if this turned out to be the case, Sunny and Karin planned to trust Benjamin and Joseph to run the school for two more weeks, while they took their holiday in Kerala, South India.

The young men were soon introduced to the Punjabi culture of North India, which is totally different to the South India culture and language (both of which Sunny had experienced himself). As he had said, it had been like moving to a totally new and different country! Both spoke Hindi and English, so there would be no problem for them communicating with the children and their families.

On Sunny and Karin's return from Kerala a *final decision would then be made. We and our friends would continue to pray and believe for the perfect outcome.* This worked out as Sunny and Karin had hoped and it seemed that Benjamin and Joseph were the right people for the job. We did feel this was of God as the *most spectacular thing was this: now for that story...*

These same young men, Benjamin and Joseph, were brought up in an orphanage in South India (*the very one)* where Sunny had worked as a volunteer after he met the Lord Jesus, some twenty years before. So they knew one another very well, although Benjamin and Joseph were still children themselves at that time. *But that's not all...for again that same orphanage was the one where Andrew Hazelden, the potter from Oxford UK. (who had introduced me to Sunny) had had a connection for many years, visiting there frequently!*

Some would say; what coincidences. I would have to say (*from my heart*) that there are no coincidences with God; all is God incidences! I am convinced, as all along this journey from the inception of House of Hope and beyond. God has used the right people at 'His Time' with 'His Wisdom' to create 'His Intricate Tapestry Design' for all of us and these needy people.

Our lives are in His Hands. Our sweet, sweet Lord, how much we love You, because You loved us before we even knew You. We can say wholeheartedly, like the disciple John,

We love *Him*, because He first loved us. 1 John 4:19 (AMP) Bible

Trust (lean on, rely on, and be confident) in the Lord and do good: so shall you dwell in the land and feed surely on His faithfulness, and truly you shall be fed.

Delight yourself also in the Lord, and He will give you the desires and secret petitions of your heart.

Commit your way to the Lord [roll and repose each care of your load on Him]; trust (lean on, rely on, and be confident) also in Him and He will bring it to pass Trust (lean on, rely on, and be confident) in the Lord and do good; so shall you dwell in the land and feed surely on His faithfulness, and truly you shall be fed. Psalm 37:3-5 (AMP) Bible

The Bible assures us God has a plan for our lives and He will fulfil it, as we trust and rest in Him. I learnt a little chorus at 'Sunday School' it goes like this:

'Jesus can never fail; What Never? No Never! And He's my Friend'.

I have proved this over and over again throughout my life. I have failed and fallen lots of times but Jesus has *never; ever... not for one moment failed me.* He will always prove to be faithful and true because that's His Character and Nature.

The urgent need now was for a teacher to tutor in Punjabi, as the mainstream secondary schools all taught in Punjabi, being situated near the village in the Punjabi State. This person would only need to teach one to two hours a day so the children could get clarity.

Another pressing need was provision of at least a snack daily for all, as the kind owners of the nearby language school could no longer continue to meet this vital need, even for the reduced number. Nevertheless we had been so blessed and thankful for all they had done until now we felt sure God would continue to meet out need. Once again praying we left all our needs before the Holy One as we waited with anticipation to see what God would do this time.

Benjamin and Joseph did a sterling job in the House of Hope, which was evident to Sunny and Karin on their return from holiday. They saw firsthand the young men's loving concern for the children; teaching the little ones and tutoring the after school group in the evenings. They showed videos also, to keep their interest while advancing their general knowledge.

The Children's Club continued to be an exciting place, filled with enthusiasm, the children loved getting involved and can clearly see the love of Jesus demonstrated in these young men's lives, as they watch over and teach them with love and compassion.

Benjamin said to me *"These children just need real unconditional love; I was brought up in an orphanage so I understand how they feel and what they need most"*. I could see he really spoke from his heart while at the same time he was very practical and efficient.

Now for the future; let's see what God will do. We wait on Him alone.

Chapter 13

Amazing Grace!

Sunny, Karin and Deborah had a wonderfully refreshing time in Kerala with Sunny's parents and needless to say Deborah was a massive hit with both her grand-parents and her uncle... They returned at the end August to the Punjab and while delighted to get back to House of Hope; it had been really tough leaving Kerala, not having any idea when they would all meet again.

Great news for 'House of Hope'

Seeing our 'needy little ones' and working with them Benjamin and Joseph felt their hearts stirred with love and compassion for them and knew they could commit to them for the longer term. Now they would carry on this pioneer work which Sunny and Karin had started and endeavour to move the project into a new phase for the 'Glory of God' alone.

Benjamin would take over the day to day running and management of the house and Joseph would be his 'right hand man' being registered with the India Government, as Chairman and Treasurer! How we thanked God.

To say we were somewhat surprised when Sunny and Karin told us they had increasingly felt that God wanted them to branch out, after their sabbatical year, to do something new and their time in Chandigarh was finished; would be an understatement!

But, I knew God's way is the only way of peace, and not only that, but success is entirely dependent on obeying His instructions whatever we may feel. The outcome would always be amazing. Naturally Sunny and Karin felt some sadness; as did we, remembering with joy how this School and Health Project started from such a 'small mustard seed' into a blooming success for the children and their families and wider community. It had indeed been a pioneering work in an area where no one had known, cared, wanted or endeavoured to change the lives of these precious children and their families. But of course God knew and He used those 'willing hands' to work His purpose out.

Together Sunny, Karin and we, had often said "no-one will ever know (only God) the wonderful plans He has for these families to bring knowledge and light into their darkness". Every day we praise and thank Him with joyful hearts, *as we prove His faithfulness.*

I was delighted to meet with the new team through Sunny and Karin on Skype in September of that year.

Reminding me of that time some five years since; when I had first met them 'face to face' at their home in India.

What an incredible God we serve.

Chapter 14

Moving Forward

As planned Sunny and Karin with little Deborah left Chandigarh for Brazil at the end of October 2014 for a well earned rest and recuperation. All our friends and supporters wished them much happiness in their future family life and wherever and whatever God had planned for them, with blessings in abundance.

In the Bible *Jesus said:*

I came that they may have *and* enjoy life, and have it in abundance (to the full, till it overflows)

John 10: 10 (Amp) Bible

He is certainly the author and finisher of our faith and the giver of abundant and enjoyable life.

Deirdre and I planned to visit House of Hope in 2015! We looked forward with awe and anticipation to see the working out of God's plans for House of Hope and knew for sure whatever God starts He will always finish well.

He says:

"For I know the plans I have for you," declares the LORD, "plans to prosper you and not to harm you, plans to give you hope and a future". Jeremiah 29:11 (N IV) Bible

Our 'God is a great big God' we have reason to hope for incredible happenings in the future.

March 2015 arrived so quickly we could hardly imagine and Deirdre and I meet in New Delhi as we had hoped. How full of anticipation we felt…

Deirdre had already met with a Charity working in Delhi and seen their work in action. She visited many of the 50 slum areas they worked in that region and learnt a lot about the various needs and innovations this Charity had implemented in their twenty-five years of working with these poor families there. This was a programme of empowerment, where the slum families were taught how to get involved and work among their neighbours to participate in education, promotion of health and hygiene, lobbying government ministers to supply clean water and electricity to their locality. This arrangement was and is very successful and many of the young people have even graduated from University and gaining progress daily.

Two wonderful friends from Mallorca, Brenda and Jackie, came with me on this trip and what a blessing they were! It was fun and so much more relaxing to share the journey and get to know one another better. How much I thanked God for this opportunity.

We three arrived at Delhi Airport around 1.30am and while the taxi whizzed us through the frantic Delhi traffic, (even at that unearthly hour) we were relieved to arrive in one piece at our Hotel. Deirdre had arranged for us to stay at her accommodation and that was an experience in itself. The house was beautifully clean and welcoming but very Colonial in style. I felt we were stepping back in time! Heavy ornate furniture with each surface littered with ornaments and trinkets and every wall covered with pictures. The bedrooms were all decorated, each with a different theme.

Jackie and I shared the first night. In this room was heavy wallpaper depicting all the various Hindu gods, in a startling bright red and orange colour, while Brenda's room had huge flowered wallpaper. Deirdre's was more sedate, (if I remember rightly) a Chinese style. We were tired by this time and slept soundly in the comfortable beds.

Next morning we were greeted with a delicious breakfast, part English and part Indian. We were offered a choice of cornflakes and cold milk, toast and jam, fresh fruits, chapatti and Indian type omelette. There was Chai, Indian tea (as we know it) or coffee. So we certainly didn't go hungry. We made a mad scramble to get to the bank for our Indian Rupees to pay the taxi-man who'd collected us from the airport the night before.

That first day we were free to sight-see the City and our guide was waiting 'at the ready' to take us on a route he had previously planned. This proved to be a great idea as we saw much more than would have been possible if we had attempted to do this on our own. He was pleasant and gave us a history lesson as we went.

Firstly we visited the Delhi Haat a great warehouse of tourist shops with every type of ornament possible, some onyx, marble, glass, silver, brass and gold, also many paintings of the gods again. There were bed linens of every type imaginable but the most interesting for us, Indian style dresses. The pant suit was greatly in evidence with exotic colours. However we soon noted that the prices were exorbitant too! Reluctantly we gave up and went for lunch. The food was good but not as tasty as I had experienced previously, possibly catering for the foreigners' palate.

Then to the famous Akshardham Hindu temple or Swaminarayan Akshardham, known as the eighth wonder of the world. This features the life of the teenage Swaminarayan and yogi and has to be seen to be fully appreciated. The image of the yogi sitting in the lotus position dominates the temple and his image plus the whole area is overlaid in gold. The opulence is incredible and carving and paintings stunning. Well worth a visit. However I personally felt an overwhelming sadness that this religion keeps so many lives trapped in fear and despair. Outside in the local vicinity was poverty beyond belief! Our driver told us that he came weekly with his whole family to worship there.

Then we drove past India Gate where there were road works and on to the Lotus Temple. This building was much less ornate surrounded on three sides by a lake and was very peaceful. An oasis in the centre of Delhi!

We caught up with Deirdre on our return, it was so good for me to see her again and introduce her to my friends. On the morrow we would go with her to meet the directors of the Charity where she had been and see their project.

Her driver arrived early next day and took us into the centre of Delhi, it was incredible and startling to realise that the slums were 'cheek by jowl' with the wealthy areas of the city. Jackie was particularly surprised by this as she will relate later.

We visited a slum near the charity's head quarters, which simply turned off that main street. On the side as we entered, a little girl was going to the toilet in the gutter. My heart sank for her! No privacy or care. We learned later that there were very few toilets for hundreds of families in the slum. However we also saw the tremendous changes that this charity had achieved in the past twenty-five years since its inception. Electricity had been installed and clean water and each of the slum houses had their own fridge outside their front door.

One of their students took us into her home, where her grandmother and brother were seated on a bed couch. In the kitchen all the stainless steel dishes and utensils were neatly stacked. The whole house was very clean and tidy and every space was well utilised.

They were most hospitable, offering us Chai. The old lady was very animated and told us she had travelled widely, to America and Europe. She showed pride in her grand-children telling us that her grandson had come second in the Bollywood singing competition, evidenced by the large cardboard 'cut out of him' at the event. He sang for us on the day which was very moving and beautiful. I could hardly take it in that they had actually achieved all this, while still living in the slum!

It was obvious any assistance to become independent

and better their position they were keen to take and make the most of their opportunity. Many had obtained loans through a special government scheme enabling them to start their own businesses. One family related how they had bought an auto-rickshaw and were working hard to achieve their dreams for the whole family.

The charity had set up groups of women from the slums to become advocates for their neighbours, so that they could encourage others to access from the government centre, free vaccines for the newborn to five year olds, preventing many dangerous diseases and lowering the death rate for these little ones. They also encouraged their (piers) to take advantage of the health clinics and health and hygiene programmes. Education was also provided for these women to teach them to lobby the government adequately for improvements to their particular area, for essentials such as more toilets etc. Similiar schemes are our dream for House of Hope in the future as God leads us.

Then it was off to Chandigarh the next day. After an uneventful flight we were met by the boys, Benjamin and Joseph while Benny had stayed at home to welcome us with his friend Pawan, (whom we named the chef) as that was in fact his profession. He cooked lots of delicious food for us during our stay.

'House of Hope' was everything I had hoped and much better than any picture could indicate. It was so good to share with the young men their dreams and aspirations and total love for God.

The younger children came in the mornings for breakfast and some conversation in English while the teachers assisting the older children after school, was working well with them having access to the House of Hope facilities, computer, books etc. and of course most importantly the Punjabi teachers helped them to understand what they had learnt at school and remembered, in their own Hindi language.

A health clinic was arranged for the following two days, this was run by Deirdre while Brenda and Jackie were essential helpers. This was a wonderful blessing to the families and children and was still in progress when I returned from Tony's home on the Tuesday evening. But I'm running ahead of myself here…

Chapter 15

My time at the Farm

I had planned with everyone (in advance) that the next day we would all meet up with Tony David in Chandigarh at a well known restaurant and get to know one another. This was a great success and Sapna, his second daughter came too. How my heart sang, to see him looking strong and in control again. It seemed only like yesterday we had been together and shared, but of course so much had happened in the interim with Pal's death and Tony's complete recovery!

It was lovely for me to chat with Tony and Sapna and catch up with family news. Rani greeted us happily with the other younger girls, Pooja and Fairy. Meenakshi was at her aunty Shanti's home. It was such a peaceful and loving atmosphere and we chatted until all were tired and ready for a good sleep. Next day I met with Akanski and her young brother both of whom spoke perfect English.

Kuldeep Tonys' nephew, was there with his beautiful wife and daughter. His brother Tushar was still working at his computer job and modeling in his spare time.

Tonys' older brother, (the boys' father) stopped by and we had a nice reunion.

My time was spent sitting around with all the older ladies in the cool sunshine or walking; constantly being chaperoned by any of the young people who happened to be free at that time. It was a real joy for me to see them all progressing with their studies and family life. I felt a whole new era had begun and it would be great.

Tony appeared somewhat preoccupied but I learned later that Meenakshi had decided she would marry her love choice and not wait for her parents arranged marriage, as was the custom!

Unusually this provided me with the unique opportunity to meet Tonys' Guru who had come at his request to help him see what God would have him do; follow tradition or be more sympathetic to the young people's need to be together; I presumed.

On arrival at the room where they were all gathered I saw Tony on his haunches with hands cupped in a pose of supplication before the Guru; who was in fact quite a young man. Tony explained to me that this was Hinduism! He then introduced me as his mother and explained how our relationship had come about because of his real mother's last request. Tony then started to explain that it was necessary for him as a good Hindu to follow tradition with regard to his daughter's proposed marriage, however his Guru could tell him if it were sinful for her to go ahead with her decision or not. He then told me some more facts about his faith and was interested to see that I had already studied Hinduism and was informed of some of their beliefs.

Meanwhile I prayed fervently in my heart that my response would be 'God given' by the power of God's Holy Spirit' so that I could present the freedom I had experienced in Jesus and how my acceptance of Jesus as the substitute for my sin; meant that I was free and fully forgiven for all time from a need to try to work my way, by *Good Karma*, until I realised 'I myself' was in fact God.

Firstly I gently explained that for me Jesus was the only Mediator between God and any human being for the Bible says:

For, there is only one God and one Mediator who can reconcile God and humanity--the man Christ Jesus.1 Timothy 2:5 NLT

Yeshua *(Jesus)* said to him, "I AM THE LIVING GOD, The Way and The Truth and The Life; no man comes to my Father but by me alone." John 14:6 Ab. Bible in plain English.

"I--yes, I alone--will blot out your sins for my own sake and will never think of them again. Isaiah 43:25 (NLT) Bible

How absolutely wonderful this is, in comparison to the belief in re-incarnation and *Karma, which would leave my heart sad, and my future in danger.*

I reflected, if true, I may have to come back many times, be re-incarnated, *never knowing* for sure, when I could or ever would, stop that cycle and become one with the God within me... Karma states there is *no forgiveness* only cause and effect...

On the other hand if the Bible is true... as I believe it is; God's word to us... clearly states:

"So also Christ died once for all time as a sacrifice to take away the sins of many people. He will come again, not to deal with our sins, but to bring salvation to all who are eagerly waiting for him."

Hebrews 9:28 (NLT) Bible

If this life is merely an illusion ... that would surely mean that the 'Creator God, is the same as His creation'... How could that be? I contemplated.

Andrew makes a pot of clay on his potter's wheel. Can

we say, he (Andrew) is the same as his pot? Obviously he is the potter and the pot is his creation ... both can never be the same, if that were so, then there is no reason or logic in anything, and if this life *is all an illusion...* what does it matter about anything; what way we live, what we do or say?... We have no control over our destiny, all is chance and self trying to become one with God or endeavour to become God.

However on the other hand the Bible declares:

In the beginning, God created the universe.

Genesis 1:1 (ISV) Bible

John, (Jesus disciple) wrote concerning Jesus calling Him the Word of God ...In *the beginning* was the Word, and the Word was with God, and the Word was God. He was in *the* beginning with God. All things came into being through Him, and without Him not even one *thing* came into being that has come into being. In Him was life, and the life was the light of men. And the Light shines in the darkness, and the darkness has not overcome it.

St.John1: 1-3 Berean Literal Bible

By the word of the LORD were the heavens made; and all the host of them by the breath of his mouth.

Psalm 33:6 (KJ) Bible

I thanked Tony for the great privilege of meeting his Guru, which I meant sincerely. However, I longed to hear the Guru's views, but he didn't speak to me in English (although he clearly understood) and I had no Hindi...I continue to pray daily that the living God will reveal Himself to both he and Tony and their families, so that they will find the peace that passes all human understanding... Not just having a 'Religion' but an amazing relationship with the living God.

Because of all this drama, Tony didn't return with me to Chandigarh but Fairy, his youngest daughter came along with our driver and Satpal (Rani's brother and his business partner) They all seemed very impressed with our 'House of Hope' but had to leave immediately to return home as it was getting late and the roads were very busy due to lots of road works, Fairy and I had an opportunity to converse together and became very close in the process.

I believe God will touch this family in a very unique way and open their eyes to see the risen Lord Jesus. I thank God for our relationship over the past almost twenty years and know God has a plan He will work to bring joy and peace to each one of them. This is my belief and unending prayer...

The days flew bye with so much to see and enjoy. God

is certainly working in 'House of Hope' to move the project forward for the benefit of all the children and their families.

We know by God's grace this is only the beginning of an amazing blessing to these families. Every day we thank God for the commitment shown by these Godly young men and their unselfish love for the children. Let's see where God leads ... we will follow for His honour alone.

'House of Hope' a dream being fulfilled

'House of Hope'... I truly feel this is a place where *hope has been born* and continues to grow daily in the lives of all who work and those who benefit from the outreach into their dire communities bringing massive hope for change and renewal in every area of life. This is indeed my prayer to God every day.

Also as I finish *for now*, this saga of *'Amazing Grace'* I would ask you to pray and believe with me for happiness and true joy and peace to be poured out on Tony David and his family. The Lord Jesus Himself the *'Bright and Morning Star'* to shine His light of love and clarity into their lives, so that they will not just have a religion like now, (which they follow avidly) but their eyes may be opened so they can share an amazing relationship of love with 'Almighty God Himself'.

As the Bible states, this gift of love is free to all who ask for forgiveness and accept Jesus as their only '*Sufficient Sacrifice*' for sin, then for them He is only a breath away…

Impressions of India by my friends

As this was the first visit to India for both Brenda and Jackie, and also Sarah and Kathi's later visits, I have asked them all to give you there initial impressions. This I think they have done admirably!

I have also included a lovely poem by Naomi, who came out on a visit to 'House of Hope', and like Katie knows India well.

A recent update from Deirdre of her second visit completes for now, these useful impressions.

Here you will find some different prospective and in some areas there will be repetition but I think it gives a fresh look at what it could be like for you should you consider a visit to India and maybe even 'House of Hope'...

Dorothy

Jackie Sowerby.

An Indian Spring of Hope

In the Spring of 2015 I was gifted the opportunity to accompany my friends Dorothy and Brenda to India, specifically to visit the capital state of Punjab Chandigarh and be a witness to the work being carried out in the slums and with children of the 'untouchables' in the 'House of Hope' school. It was amazing to see this being done, selflessly, by Indian doctors, teachers and their staff. Sometimes harrowing, sometimes sad but ultimately rewarding to see the improvement in the lives of those living in poverty. I felt humbled to see these poor children access free education, health and an opportunity to see the love of God in action.

A snapshot of my trip

We are here!

Having left the sunny Isle of Mallorca one morning, after seemingly endless airport terminals, we arrived in Delhi in the early hours of the following day. We were met by three wonderful young men who are working in the 'House of Hope' in Chandigarh Straight away we could see how engaging they were and how 'fired up' to serve the Lord. As I would see through my trip this was a recurring theme of service, humility and contentment...but against some incredible challenges.

However, I am getting ahead of myself! Having been born in Manila I thought I would have been better prepared for the heat, the exhaust fumes and the noise of a large city. But wow, what an onslaught on my senses!

In many respects it was a feeling of 'deja vu'. I felt I had been transported back 20 years to the Philippines, just it seemed even crazier than Manila. The drivers don't obey any traffic rules.

They drive forward without a thought of looking left or right, it seemed as though somebody was looking after them. It appeared that the one behind was guarding the one in front, or maybe it is just 'an Indian solution to an Indian problem', i.e. somewhere in the apparent chaos there is order arising from it...a miracle every day?

First impressions

The people were so hospitable, respectful and generally despite the challenges were very happy. I could see a lot of similarities between the Philippines and India regarding agriculture, traditions, mentality and culture. They are wonderfully family orientated. It made me feel glad...like being at home.

Sadly the similarities extended to the social and political challenges faced by many emerging nations with people from the country flocking to the cities. The gap between the 'haves' and the 'have nots' is so much wider than we see in western society. The government or the social and religious groups seemed impotent in moving the class society forward.

The culture: The diversity of social, economic and religious groupings was striking. Many different languages are spoken and so many various religious beliefs exist side by side. Hindu, Buddhist, Muslim, Sikh and Christians all seem to co-exist peacefully.

India is a class ridden society with a rich higher class, a middle 'technocrat' class and at the bottom is what can only be described as an underclass; or 'the untouchables'. To those of us in the West this class or caste system will touch our sensibilities, but we should not judge without understanding it fully first...better we leave that to a higher power!

I got the impression that underpinning all these belief systems was a fatalistic view that this was what life had dealt them and they were contented with their lot. However, as I was to witness despite these differences there is a lot of inter social help given through various social projects.

The challenges India faces: - I thought I had seen slums in the Philippines and Mexico but the area we visited left me lost for words. One particular community we visited in Patiala had more than 2000 people living with no running water, no sanitation. Their children didn't attend any real school because most of them have no birth certificates (without which they cannot attend school).

Many people when you asked them how old they were, they simply did not know!

We all hear of and see parts of India that are so beautiful with rich architecture, high tech business parks, foreign business call centers and a young population that is well educated and forward thinking.

But these opportunities are not for all! If you are born as an untouchable (effectively an outcast) then you will struggle to overcome the prejudice of your countrymen.

Thankfully we see God working in many areas of Indian society, ironically supported by many members of society who hold these same prejudices. It just shows that underneath we all are gifted with a sense of right and wrong and are presented with an opportunity to make a difference. We can pray that the Holy Spirit will work to bring about a change in attitude towards the under privileged.

Special People:- I was humbled to witness the help given by a pastor and his wife in Patiala. They go a few days every week to run a school camp and an occupational health camp inside the slums. It is hard to forget Pastor Akash and his wife Manju, who is a nurse. They carried themselves with such grace. You could see that in their hearts they only had a desire to help the people in the slums and share with them the love of Jesus.

They get no help from outside India and exist purely on support within the neighbourhood, through bags of maize, rice, and other necessary commodities.

Hope! So what are our 3 young gentlemen welcome committee doing? We had by now travelled to the outskirts of Chandigarh where they serve in the 'House of Hope'. This is a charitable organisation that runs a school aimed at kids with ages ranging from 2 years to 13 years

The children attending the school are almost exclusively from the untouchable class. This means they are regarded as the lowest of the low in society. Almost all will have no birth certificate, (until now) which is a requirement to go to a state school. Later in life they will not be able to get a passport...imagine we take travel and freedom of movement for granted, but these people will probably never see anything other than their country homes or maybe even worse the slums of Chandigarh.

Many are of Punjabi and Hindu background, but here in the 'House of Hope' they learn English and get an opportunity to see God's love for them.

My heart was almost broken when I saw one 10 year old boy who was deaf and could not speak. He was looking after his younger brother and could not attend school. Every morning he would come to the staff house before the classes start to try and learn what he could. Without a miracle this young boy cannot attend the special school he needs. This is such a shame as he is very artistic.

All around the world we witness great charities at work, doing good works in disaster areas, medical assistance, education, etc. I have been privileged to see a much more personal approach to helping others.

I find myself thinking what can I do to help these young people who do not have the education, health care, and living conditions that my own children enjoy? I can ask for prayer that India and its people do not forget their own.

However I know that God will meet them where they are and will love them equally.

Brenda Stephens

The accessibility of media resources today educates us in the great needs that exist all over the world caused by either natural disasters or circumstances of life. When children are involved, our automatic response is to protect the young and vulnerable.

Dorothy had previously shared the history that led up to the establishing of the 'House of Hope' with our women's group and it became the desire of my heart to visit India and meet the leaders, helpers, children and family members involved. So, when the opportunity to go and see for myself became a reality, I jumped at the chance.

I had questions, of course – such as, why is it important for me to go, and what do I hope to achieve? How do I prepare myself for a new mysterious culture with all its differences in dress, food and goals? How would I cope with the inequality between the...haves and the have nots? What will God direct me to do during and after such a visit?

I felt both excited and insecure about the journey to Chandigarh.

I left with Dorothy and Jackie and we met up with Deirdre (a Doctor) in Delhi. I'm glad to share about some days from the trip, which were moving, thrilling and poignant, all containing moments I will never forget.

We arrived in Delhi in the early hours of Friday. The large hotel bed looked very inviting and not even a painful back affected my sleep!

My initial impressions of Delhi were that it was bigger than I'd imagined and in the areas we travelled, the roads were also better than I'd expected. The buildings were a mixture of both modern and less well developed. The food was surprisingly English! Our agenda was to explore the area, so equipped with our rupees, we set out.

The volume of traffic had increased from the early hours and the first thing that struck us, was the constant cacophony of horns used to tell other drivers to get out of the way! Two traffic lanes were somehow crammed into five. It didn't seem as though indicators were ever used, so it was impressive that everyone came out unscathed – usually!

We were privileged to have Pramod as our tour guide and taxi driver for the afternoon and he was ready with a list of attractions for us to see, one of which was The Bahai Lotus Temple. This was a temple of prayer, a stunning building in the shape of a lotus flower. The inside was spacious and the acoustics would have been amazing for a choir. The grounds were both beautiful and peaceful.

Our next stop after fighting through the traffic the

Delhi Haat. This was a craft area and restaurant. The craft stalls were very intriguing, offering articles that captivated the imagination especially considering the dexterity and skill required to achieve the final results. We also looked at the colourful long dress tunics that were on show and worn on an everyday basis by the ladies.

Our first Indian meal contained a selection of dishes - Tikka Masala, Mutton and Veggie rice. It was very good but this was when I learnt what spiced food really was in no uncertain terms! I finished with a yogurt drink to counter the heat in my mouth – though everyone else seemed to be fine!

Our last call was to the Aksherdham Temple, a Hindu place of worship. The architecture was amazing - not a place to be forgotten and extremely popular with families and tourists.

Our first day tired us out, so we returned to base and met up with Dr. Deirdre. Our evening meal together was rice, veggie curry (not too hot), lentil soup, tomatoes, onions and bread. With an agreed 9am pick up for the next day, we settled down early for the night.

Saturday
Asha House in Delhi, is a charitable organisation supporting 50 plus slums in their local area (Asha means, "Hope" in Hindi). Anurag spoke about the work and we were taken to the school to meet the teachers and

children who gave us a lovely flower petal greeting.

They have a team of committed teachers and volunteers who give unconditionally to the work needed for those in their care. Their love for all the children was evident in everything they did and said. The volunteers encouraged mothers to become involved and as a group, to speak with Government officials making them aware of their problems and need for practical and financial support.

Some of the children spoke about themselves and their school responsibilities. They were lively and excited to meet us. A few managed a little English whilst others were overcome with shyness but chatted via translation. The aim of the school was not only to give them an education but a pride in themselves, their surroundings and others, which was very clearly producing results.

We visited one slum home where the Grandmother was present. The home was shared with several generations of family members and consisted of two main rooms. Grandma was amazing – she told us how proud she was of her children and grand-children, one of whom was attending college and giving her spare time to the 'Hands of Hope School'.

Thinking back on this visit it's hard to grasp that these children were actually living in slum conditions. I think I expected them to look less clean and spruced up and it was only when we had a short glimpse of the slum area surrounding them, that I realized how much care had already been given to this one small group.

Our next visit was the 'House of Hope' in Chandigarh.

We were met by Benjamin and Joseph two amazing guys. Their love for God and desire to give of themselves to the children in their care was outstanding. To help them achieve this were some teachers, volunteers, and a cleaner all of whom we were able to meet.

The 'House of Hope' offers both accommodation for teachers and visitors and is also a school for children. It is a compact building with adequate rooms, kitchen and sluice (bucket and jug) shower. It consisted of three floors. We were made to feel extremely welcome and comfortable. Our meal was a takeaway Indian Tandoori chicken and rice, (spicy!) and we took the opportunity to get to know everyone before resting that night and the Sunday.

Monday to Wednesday

This was our opportunity to meet the children and spend time with them. They were very curious and just wanted to be near us. Some of them wandered into the home area of the school and were treated just like extended family members, never being turned away. All the leaders and helpers had positive relationship with each child and when hearing the history of different children it became very apparent that over the years these children been hugely helped in every area of their lives.

Some needs were more obvious than others. For example, one young boy who was deaf and dumb and very intelligent would have benefited from a special course in sign language.

An advantage to others would have been one to one support. More personal care for the slightly older children would have been profitable for the years ahead.

The commitment of those caring giving of their love unstintingly to the children and their families, was an example to all.

We held a clinic for both children and parents enabling us to look at basic health issues. Their response was extremely positive. It allowed us to record details of each persons' name, age, previous injections; height, weight, body mass and blood pressure and for Doctor Deidre to check their general health and any medication required.

This was our last day at Chandigarh and the whole visit had been an amazing experience.

The children gave a presentation of singing and thanks. We all received flowers and cards and even though this had been a short visit I felt as though I had grown closer to the children. They had really touched my heart.

The team were amazing, nothing was too much trouble. They cooked for us again (another type of curry, still spicy - but God bless yoghurt!) My head was asleep before it hit the pillow.

Special visit

Pastor Akash and his wife welcomed us and told us a little of their story and work. They had adopted 5 of the slum children who lived with them in their family unit and without question their hearts and lives were totally given over to the people in the slum areas and to any person in need.

We were taken to the local town where we were greeted by approximately 60 people all waiting to attend a clinic, which we were asked to run. We were presented with a couple of tables, some paper, a blood pressure machine and a selection of medications and for the next three hours we attended to all present repeating all that we had done in the school.

A team of nurses were on hand to administer intravenous fluids to the dehydrated patients and we had cases of tuberculosis, cataracts, strokes, rickets and malnutrition. Many patients asked for prayer and it broke my heart when I prayed for a young girl with tuberculosis who I later saw in the slum area at home with her parents. Here was another obvious need for increasing preventative and active health care for all ages.

This was followed by a visit to the Patila slum area and words cannot describe the situation. The children, (happy as children can be in the only situation they know) were underfed, wearing clothes that they had slept in for months. Most of them looked like they hadn't seen water on their bodies or hair for years. They were lacking in basic living facilities with little or no education. There was limited water supply and no electricity.

The government has indicated that they may put electric light into an area which would facilitate it, but there is no sign of any change except for the possibility of people being moved on as the need for property development becomes a greater requirement. Their living space was in waste grounds amongst wrecked cars, broken machines, scrap metal, just about anything you could think of. Access was via muddy rough tracks, full of puddles. Their homes consisted of bits of covering over poles and pieces of wood for beds. They cooked over open fires.

The Pastor told us he had bought a plot of land and had already built the walls for a church, school and children's home. That very week he was planning to introduce his first small group of children to meet for a teaching fun session under the shelter of a canopy.

I am in no doubt that those involved with the care of these children seek God with all their hearts and minds as to the work they are involved in. It was a joy and a privilege to share a little time with both children and carers and I felt extremely humbled by the whole experience

So how did my visit enable me to answer my original questions?

I am in no doubt that it was right for me to go as it enabled me to appreciate how blessed I am in Mallorca and how I take the provisions of life so much for granted.

Accepting the mysteries of different cultures, religions, dress, food etc was made easy as everyone we met were gracious and respectful. They received us with joy and always offered the very best they had.

The diversity between the wealthy and poor was very obvious. There is rejection of slum children. There is a huge need for government, religious and charitable organisations to work together and pour resources into providing practical accommodation and basic living facilities. Opportunities need to be created in order to develop skills for self-achievement and independence.

I believe that God has provided us with a world that is sufficient for all our needs. Many of us have far more than we need, whilst others have so little. This is not only in the financial or material area of life but, in how we use our time.

What is Gods direction for me with regard to this visit?

I have become so much more aware of what I have and am considering ways in which I can be of benefit to others in a much deeper sense. I continue to seek Gods direction regarding sad situations that face us in the world today.

Anyone who has to rummage in bins or a waste area to get food or water, or beg on the streets and have no bed to lay their heads on at night, will tug at my heart.

None of us knows when or if, our lifestyles could change or if we might even find ourselves facing challenges like these. You may think it very unlikely, but if it did happen, I wonder how you or I would cope?

Sarah Beckett

I was fortunate to spend a week at the 'House of Hope' in March last year and I really treasure the time I had there. Never having visited a place so far removed from my own culture, all the colours and sounds were so interesting to me. One of the things that really stood out was the overwhelming warmth, both of the 'House of Hope' team and of all the Indian families we met. One of the days was spent visiting the families in the slums around the 'House of Hope'. It was a humbling experience and I have never felt so welcomed. The sense of community between the families living in such close proximity was tangible. Whilst the parents were working the children all looked after each other.

Afterwards, I couldn't help thinking that although the society I live in is so incredibly privileged, the communities I saw in India seem to have an interdependence that we have lost in London, where I live. Another thing that really struck me was the total faith in God exhibited by the 'House of Hope' team. I found it incredible the way they would start projects without a clear idea of how things would work out but with complete trust that they would somehow manage. More incredible was they always did work things out, one way or another.

The impact of the 'House of Hope' is so tangible when you are there to see it first hand and I would highly recommend a visit. It is the kind of project with real, on the ground and immediate effect that is so worthwhile to support.

Dr.Deirdre Shawe

Impressions of a second visit to the 'House of Hope', Chandigarh, India: March 2015

I first visited the House of Hope School in April 2014, having combined it with a trip to Pakistan. I was impressed by the great need of the slum community in Chandigarh, but also the enormously positive impact the school was already having on the children and their families. I left with a much clearer idea of how to help in financial and medical terms, and the hope that I would be able to return.

The opportunity came in March 2015. I travelled initially to Delhi where I spent a week working voluntarily as a doctor for an Indian charity known as Asha. This charity, started 25 years ago by Dr Kiran Martin, provides education and health care to some of the slum communities in Delhi. Here I got a clearer vision of what could be done at the 'House of Hope'. The model of Asha, which has transformed the lives of many families living in poverty in Delhi, was what I thought could be achieved eventually in Chandigarh, albeit on a smaller scale.

To the outsider, India seems a chaotic place. The roads are packed full of battered vehicles, animals, people and motorised rickshaws. Car horns sound constantly and the street are littered with rubbish. There is some order in the chaos however. The rickshaws are an efficient and cheap way of getting around and my work in the slum clinics became more fruitful when I realised I could purchase any drugs needed for the patients from local pharmacies. I found the pharmacists to be helpful and well informed: a drug that was not in stock could be ordered and arrived within a few hours on a motorbike!

Arriving at the 'House of Hope', with Dorothy Thompson and two friends was exciting. We were made to feel most welcome. I was impressed by the commitment to the project of the two young men who were now in charge. They seemed to have a maturity beyond their years and demonstrated, in their way of living, that God was their strength day to day. We were able to help in practical terms with cleaning at the school, spending time with some of the children and running several medical clinics.

One of these was in Patiala, a nearby town, where the slum community lived in the worst conditions I had witnessed, with only tents as housing and no toilets. A local pastor had set up a small school there, with some limited health care. A single stand pipe had been installed to provide water, the year previously. Here we found ourselves having to run a medical camp with about a hundred expectant patients awaiting our arrival.

There was a wealth of pathology, including tuberculosis, malnutrition and deformed limbs due to untreated fractures. A number of older people complained of poor vision but their sight was restored when I lent them my glasses! We left appropriate prescriptions, which would be paid for by the pastor, and were reminded of the many advantages of modern health care systems such as the NHS in the UK!

Our efforts seemed like a drop in the ocean of the vast poverty in India, much aggravated by the inequality in that society. It is also true to say, however, that a little bit goes a long way in India and we were humbled but also inspired to continue the work of helping the 'House of Hope' Project.

Kathi Borchmann

India this colourful, beautiful country where I stayed for 8 months touched me in many ways. Especially as there is so much to see and experience that you will never find in Europe; spicy food, different tastes and people that want you to come to their home and to serve you food and tea.

The Indians are friendly very open to us. Sometimes the foreigner may find this familiarity a bit too much, for instance, in their culture it isn't rude to stop and stare at you openly...follow you around and ask you hundreds of questions!

They say we like your white skin... as to them fair skin is so beautiful and they endeavour not to spend too much time in the sun so they will not get too brown, while we,(on the whole) luxuriate in the chance to sit in the sun whenever possible...Taking pictures with you all the time so that 'you are in the spotlight' can be very disconcerting, as they want to be near you and give you their full attention.

However I was impressed by the Indian hospitality and kindness.

It's interesting to see everywhere so crowded, full of

people and action and in every corner it smells different.

It can be quite dirty in the streets compared to my home country Germany. In general you hear a lot of loud noises, cars beeping and the traffic seems in our eyes like total chaos...

Cows which are held sacred and other animals and different kinds of vehicle are here, there and everywhere.

You will find it best if you can be relaxed and go with the flow...whatever you do or whatever will happen and take your time, as the Indians do the same...then you will adapt and get used to this different pace of life.

In India you see extreme poorness of the society and at the same time you see the very rich society nearby. As this country is so big and diverse, it can be shocking for the people from outside Asia to see both strata's of society in such close proximity.

Knowing God is control in everything; I survived the experience of India and found it quite an adventure, as of course we come from a completely different Country.

A Poem by: Naomi Hargreaves.

The children arrive at House of Hope
they are young and disheveled,
How do they cope?
Roaming the streets with no parents in sight
to fend for themselves, this is their plight.

The children are from the lowest caste
whatever happens they're always last
Rejected, abandoned, who is to blame?
The "untouchables", this is their name.

Along came Benjamin and Joseph
Full of God's love wherever they go!
They gathered the children from far and wide
And began to work, with God by their side...

School is provided every day
the children are taught how to pray
English and Punjabi are on the list
and maths. and reading isn't missed

They're eager to learn and full of life
A moment away from their troubles and strife
they're given time, attention and care
At 'House of Hope' God's love is there

The children have nothing and yet they're so glad
The Government don't help and that makes me mad
But we are the ones who can lend a hand
Together we can make a stand

For we can all give, even a prayer
we can help see their lives turned around
Asking for nothing and yet needing so much
Will you, be the one to provide a touch

of care and concern, for the littlest of these?
If you spend time with them, you can hear their pleas
Help us and teach us, we need you to care
Will you be the ones who with us you'll share?

Consider today what you can give
To help a small child in our world
live!
Whatever you do for the least of
these
You do it for God and He is pleased.

Katie Mc Donald

My first experience of India was during my second year at university when I was offered an exchange with Pearl academy of Fashion in Delhi. During my month studying there, I researched the textiles industry in Gujarat, which was a magical 45 hour train journey from Delhi.

Each village had its own traditional craft, from block printing to embroidery, bell making and weaving. It was fascinating to meet the makers and talk to them about how their craft has developed over the years, and how they keep up with the ever changing design market. We researched and worked with them in order to help their sales, giving them advice on new trends and ideas for creating sellable items from their craft. I really loved their slower pace of life and sense of community, which coming from London, I had never experienced before.

The exchange came to an end, but after a month, I had fallen in love with India and refused to leave! I changed my flights and visa and got in touch with designers in Delhi, seeking out more work to keep me in this beautiful country longer. I was blessed with an internship with a successful designer called Nitin Bal Chauhan.

Nitin was inspired by the small details in everyday life,

looking up at the tangled wires and telegraph poles, or details in nature - and turning them into beautiful prints and embroideries. What I loved most about his work was his links with craftsmen, and how he combined their work with his to give them a better income.

Most of the artists were based in Himachal Pradesh, where I spent a week at the end of my internship in a beautiful town called Shimla. We created a collection for India Fashion Week, and I worked with the pattern cutters and factories to make our drawings a reality. It was a really exciting time, and the peoples way of life and beautiful nature has stayed with me ever since.

My fascination with India and textiles has always been there, but life and work took over and I didn't get back into designing for years, life took me out to sea instead, due to a lack of work in the UK. I joined the world of super yachts and based myself between the Caribbean and Mallorca, where I met Dorothy and Peter at Santa Ponca Church. Our shared love of Jesus and India made us instant friends, and we have been ever since! Dorothy started telling me about 'House of Hope', and her time spent in Chandigarh with Benjamin and Joseph, two inspirational young men, who run a safe haven for children who have grown up in slum areas. I knew that

God was calling me to go back to India, but kept putting it off. I was focusing on my career on boats, but God had other plans and the soon the yacht I worked on ended up in a storm, which cracked the hull, leaving the boat stuck in Cornwall right next to a wonderful church called Harbour. My faith grew and soon I was getting prophetic words from the pastor about my heart for children in India and mission work, and I knew that my heart was longing to go back. I asked God to give me an obvious sign as to when I should go to 'House of Hope', and that afternoon I received a call from an old friend inviting me to Sri Lanka for a week, and that she had found an incredibly cheap one way flight from London.

This was the start of my adventure from the very south of India, up to my final destination in Chandigarh. I travelled from Sri Lanka to Kerela, where I lived with the most amazing family on the backwaters, where I spent some quiet time with God, and prayed into my time at 'House of Hope', asking God how he wanted to use me to bless these children and families.

I then flew to Chandigarh where I met Benjamin and Joseph, and their amazing church family who instantly welcomed me with wonderful hospitality, delicious food and lots of laughter. For the first two weeks the children were on their school holidays, which meant they had a lot of free time and energy! I spent this precious time with them teaching them to draw and paint. I chose bible verses which I felt would be useful for their lives and taught them to write creatively and draw around the verses. Some amazingly talented artists emerged and so many proud faces as they showed me their creations.

I was lucky to work alongside Joel, Benjamin's younger brother from Goa, who communicated so well with the children in Hindi, and translated for me. Each verse had a story which he taught them about, and it was so amazing to see them listen and learn about Jesus, and how having a relationship with him can change their life.

When the children went back to school, I taught the teachers embroidery, which was a lot of fun, and I hope that creative skill can be passed down to the children too. I loved the slow pace of life at 'House of Hope', and how much love this family had for one another.

The children had such close friendships and you could tell that they cared deeply for each other, even when play fighting! I saw them as rays of light and they gave me so much hope, knowing that they had firm foundations in Jesus. It was amazing to hear stories of conversions and how the simple gospel has simplified their lives, rules have been thrown out and replaced with peace and love.

I felt so privileged to have spent some time with this amazing family, and to see God's work in providing for them in miraculous ways, it really strengthened my faith.

I stayed at 'House of Hope' for 5 weeks, and it was the most blessed time. I felt so at home, I went there planning to show love to the children, but ended up receiving so much love myself, more than I could have imagined.

The community was outrageously generous and loving towards me. I really enjoyed visiting their homes, and I was often invited for amazing dinners with their families, or for tours of each child's home, which was a real privilege. Those were very precious times which I will never forget.

I have started my own small design company in Cornwall, selling luxury silk scarves with prints of my photographs and paintings. I plan to continue to support them through my design work.

Further Books available: Dorothy Fallows -Thompson:

Children's Fiction: '*New Adventures in the 'Garden of Secrets'*'

Also Written under Pen Name: Cynthia Myles:

Children's Fiction: '*Jimmy's Best Christmas Ever*'

Adult Fiction: '*At the End of the Rainbow*'

#0060 - 121217 - C0 - 210/148/8 - PB - DID2061953